THE Dyn… OF PO…ERFUL PARENTING

a human nature approach

RAYMOND MESSER, MSW
PSYCHOTHERAPIST AND PARENT EDUCATOR

Note for Librarians: a cataloguing record for this book that includes Dewey Decimal Classification and US Library of Congress numbers is available from the Library and Archives of Canada. The complete cataloguing record can be obtained from their online database at:
www.collectionscanada.ca/amicus/index-e.html
ISBN 1-4120-5314-5

TRAFFORD

Offices in Canada, USA, Ireland and UK

This book was published *on-demand* in cooperation with Trafford Publishing. On-demand publishing is a unique process and service of making a book available for retail sale to the public taking advantage of on-demand manufacturing and Internet marketing. On-demand publishing includes promotions, retail sales, manufacturing, order fulfilment, accounting and collecting royalties on behalf of the author.

Book sales for North America and international:
Trafford Publishing, 6E–2333 Government St.,
Victoria, BC V8T 4P4 CANADA
phone 250 383 6864 (toll-free 1 888 232 4444)
fax 250 383 6804; email to orders@trafford.com
Book sales in Europe:
Trafford Publishing (UK) Ltd., Enterprise House, Wistaston Road Business Centre,
Wistaston Road, Crewe, Cheshire CW2 7RP UNITED KINGDOM
phone 01270 251 396 (local rate 0845 230 9601)
facsimile 01270 254 983; orders.uk@trafford.com
Order online at:
trafford.com/05-0209

10 9 8 7 6 5 4 3 2

Parenting is about training the next generation of parents; parenting should not be about the business of inflicting needless pain to create fear as a way to shape behavior.

This book is dedicated to my families, past and present, and to the families with whom I have met and worked during my career.

THE BASIC TRUTH OF EFFECTIVE PARENTING

–our goal is to work yourself out of a job in about eighteen years.

It's not easy; but it is doable. This book will help.

It's written by a parent, and a counselor of parents and children who have learned to overcome seemingly insurmountable obstacles.

The path you'll walk is difficult—no doubt about it; an open mind is definitely required. But the potential rewards are large.

Prepare yourself to be challenged, encouraged, prodded, and motivated into a new way of relating to and parenting your child.

TABLE OF CONTENTS

ACKNOWLEDGEMENTS

This book is the product of the efforts of a number of people who have contributed, either directly or indirectly to my development, but most specifically:

My parents, who by providing me a model from which to start my journey, taught me that parents don't give up on their kids, no matter what. My wife, Nancy, who through her willingness to struggle with me to become a better husband, father and step-father, showed me the way to the joy of truly loving other people. My daughters and step-sons, who through their ongoing efforts to be themselves, taught me the joy of second place, as well as lessons in the power of love, forgiveness and the gift of a fresh start. My friend and mentor Howard Fink, Ph. D., who through his patience and wisdom, helped me learn that being a "family man" is as much about seeing and understanding as it is about knowing and doing. And finally, my clients, who through their confidence in my practice, taught me what it means to be a meaningful part of a community.

Thank you. It is my sincerest wish that this book will be a fitting tribute to each of you.

Ray Messer

EDITOR'S PREFACE

This book is worth your time.

The principles described here are not abstract musings from an armchair psychologist who imagines what it "ought" to be like for parents and children; rather, Raymond G. Messer's *Dynamics of Powerful Parenting* is an unusual blend of theory and practice. Reading just a few pages will convince you that you hold a book that can help you change how you parent, how you feel about your child and yourself, and how your child feels about you.

The illustrations come from the author's years of seasoned experience counseling parents and children — and from his own experience as husband and father. The principles herein are hard-won dictates that are born of common sense and decades of observation, years of working with troubled teens and troubled parents.

In short Ray Messer knows what he's talking about.

You will, too, after you read this book.

Will this be a life-changing experience for you? Possibly. But as you'll see in these pages, the dynamics are about *parenting,* not about changing children.

You, as the parent, have some work to do.

But it will be worth the time and effort. You'll find your child reacting differently as you handle old problems in a new way. You may even find that you can relax a bit, begin to enjoy your relationship with your child.

Sound impossible?

I thought so, too. But then I read the book. As an editor, yes, but also as the parent of a troubled teen.

Things are not perfect in my world, not by a long shot. But things are better.

And they can be better for you, too.

Gregg Sewell,
Editor

FOREWORD

The book you hold in your hand is visible proof that a man can learn from his mistakes.

The Dynamics of Powerful Parenting began as an effort to construct a simple study guide for parents who have entrusted their children's mental health and emotional well-being to my care. As work on the guide progressed, it grew into what you have in your hands. *Dynamics* is my attempt to codify the elements of successful and effective parenting as learned within my practice of psychotherapy.

Parenting is a job that we often perform without much thought or apprehension until things go awry. Everyone seems to get her chance at parenting, and each of us think we can do the job well. Criticism of another's parenting techniques is considered the height of rudeness in our society. It is taboo to address another person about the way his child behaves when that child isn't behaving well. For this reason *Dynamics* will be hard for many parents to read. While reading this book you may recall many of your past attempts at parenting as having been ineffective; don't lose heart. *Dynamics* not only offers insights to mistakes but insights to solutions as well.

What is it about parenting that makes us so defensive about the outcomes of our efforts? What is it that makes many people so closed off to information about child-rearing? Why do children's magazines seem to focus on cute babies, rather than raucous teens? What transforms that "little bundle of joy" into a youngster who climbs out of a window at night, gets caught drinking at age sixteen, gets pregnant, or is involved in a shooting?

Why are we unwilling to speak up while in line at the supermarket, when we see a small child being hit or chastised by an angry parent, yet willing to pay for these parents' mistakes by funding our prison and welfare systems? Why do we, as a society, do so little to provide education to those who are about to become parents; how can it be that a job as important as parenting requires no license or formal training?

Dynamics is written for everyone who has ever asked these and other questions. It is a culmination of nearly three decades of observation, study, and practice in the art of raising children.

The perspectives in *Dynamics* come from my daily walk with parents and children. It's not a "how to" book; it's a "why is" book. You'll learn about the dynamics of how you relate to your child and how your child relates to you—two very different things, as you will see.

Armed with this knowledge, you'll find new energy for handling one of the most invigorating, challenging, and important tasks that life can give.

— *RGM*

INTRODUCTION

Whatever you may have been told to the contrary, parenting is about power; it is about the power that you hold over your child, and the power your child holds over you in the form of victimhood (child = victim = parental guilt) and unacceptable behaviors. Most people don't want to think of parenting as a power-oriented endeavor, yet this perspective can prove quite enlightening. Most parents are not taught to be effective power brokers, and the result is a sense of frustration, despair, and wasted effort.

Parenting is about training a child to follow the basic laws of social convention and cultural propriety. Children who become "good people" must be taught how to meet their own needs in an acceptable manner within the context of their societal world. How they go about doing this is intimately related to how they are raised. In the movie *Twelve Angry Men,*[1] a brash, rude, and shallow man flippantly questions a well-mannered gentleman of European extraction where he "got his lofty manners." The gentleman's reply? "From the same place as you; it's how I was raised."

Effective parenting is about the successful teaching and learning of the important lessons of life: that life is painful, and that pain can be an opportunity for learning. The pain that life brings is inescapable; it does not consider socioeconomic status or station in life. An effective parent learns to master the art of imparting the above notions to a child without undo harshness or angry control.

Attempting to raise a child in a pain-free environment does the greatest of disservices to a child (aside from abuse or neglect) in that the child will come to expect life to be pain-free. Worse still, the child who is raised this way will come to think that it is the responsibility and duty of others to make it so. This is one reason that the divorce rate is at nearly fifty percent; partners have come to expect that life should be easier than it is, and when it proves otherwise, the spouse is blamed for the difficulties.

On the other hand, the use of pain (punishment) as the principle means for teaching and disciplining a child does another great disservice: it creates fear and anger within the child, and neither angry nor frightened children grow up to be effective, well-tempered adults.

In a sense parenting is everything. While nature provides the basic template for the personality of the individual, parenting provides the direction and "programming" that transforms a child's personality into character, which in turn will reveal the quality of the parental inputs.

All too often psychotherapy and counseling are necessary to help struggling adults cope with the damage done by angry, insensitive, and just

---

[1]Paramount Pictures, *Twelve Angry Men.*

plain mean parents. Wilhelm Reich, the father of modern character analysis once said that "psychotherapy is a good way to make a living, however, true societal change can only come from improved treatment of our children."[2] There is a reason that so many therapists and counselors are making a good living and that reason is "bad parenting." The best way to improve the quality of our social world is to improve the quality of our parenting (the irony of this assertion is that many parents will require therapy to become better parents).

Many professionals have devoted their lives to the study of parenting and to teaching parents how to deal with children and their very difficult behaviors. Often, these professionals provide a service called "parent training" or "parent education," and the efforts of these professionals are praiseworthy. What is different about *Dynamics* is a focus on parent awareness rather than parent education; much of this book has the parent looking inward at the self, rather than outward at the child.

Dynamics represents a blend of various theories of human development with elements of "plain old human nature," and human nature is very much about gaining, having and using power. The art of wielding power is the art of getting people to do what one wants them to do. Successful and effective parenting is the art of wielding personal power within the family for the success and benefit of the family as a whole, as well as its individual members.

Parenting styles vary from person to person; they can range from very strict and militaristic to very lax and deferential. In the end, no matter what the style, people in the family system will vie for power; how they go about it and how those attempt are handled by the parents will determine in large measure the quality of their lives together, and the quality of the lives of generations not yet born.

---

[2]*Reich Speaks on Freud;* pp. 46-47.

THE PRINCIPLES OF POWERFUL PARENTING

PRINCIPLE 1

Both parents must be willing to give love to another and give up the expectation of being loved in return.

PRINCIPLE 2

Mothers and fathers need to work in concert together for the benefit of their children. When they do not, their children easily become weapons in their fight against one another.

PRINCIPLE 3

Parents control the environment and set the limits of the child's freedom. The earlier a parent learns the art of being powerless over a child, the easier the job of parenting.

PRINCIPLE 4

The word 'No' *is far and away the single most important word in a child's vocabulary. Its importance is equally divided between the child's ability to both give and receive it.*

PRINCIPLE 5

Become the most important person in your child's life, but do this because the child is the most important person in your life.

PRINCIPLE 6

A parent must be confident and able to tolerate negative feelings from a child. An attitude of confidence and assurance must be transmitted to a child, especially from toddlerhood on. Confident parenting will yield confident children.

PRINCIPLE 7

Anger is the fire that tempers character; this anger should come from the child, not the parent.

PRINCIPLE 8

In family situations, most people don't behave much differently than they feel. This is especially true for children. Forcing a child to "behave" when she or he feels otherwise leads to a child who learns to avoid feeling as a way to escape punishment. This results in an adult who will have great difficulty with future family situations.

PRINCIPLE 9

There is never any need to intentionally shame a child; life is a harsh taskmaster and will yield numerous failures; rest assured, there will be more than enough shame along the way for the child to "learn his lesson."

PRINCIPLE 10

Temperance is learned by example and experience, not taught by way of instruction, criticism or insistence.

PRINCIPLE 11

Power compensates for and alleviates the shame that accompanies failure. Never underestimate an angry child's desire to thwart a parent's authority. If the only power a child can experience is the power to upset or anger the parent, then that is what he will do; neither punishments, consequences, nor self-suffering will deter the angry child.

PRINCIPLE 12

Parents should limit their expectations to what can actually be achieved; expecting children to conform with a parent's ideal of what a child should be and do is a sure way to experience heartache and frustration. Eliminate the phrase "do it because I said so" from your vocabulary. It's a waste of time and energy.

PRINCIPLE 13

A mother's power in a child's world is the power of love; a mother's use of anger rarely creates fear in a child, but instead leaves a child feeling anxious, inadequate and concerned that "mother doesn't love me anymore." A mother must find a way to discipline her child while maintaining an attitude of approval and love.

PRINCIPLE 14

Fathers should refrain from the use of anger or fear as a way of controlling a child or teaching him a lesson; anger-oriented parenting results in a child who is unable to think clearly, thus compromising his ability to "learn his lesson."

PRINCIPLE 15

Parents need to be aware that their children must experience the ability to "win" in the child-parent relationship; this victory must be fostered by the parent within reasonable tolerances for limits and boundaries. This creates a feeling of success within the child and results in less need for achieving power for power's sake (Principle #11).

PRINCIPLE 16

'Yes' *is far more powerful a motivator than any threat, coercion or punishment can ever be. Use it wisely with conditions and with sincerity. Avoid punishments for noncompliance at all costs.*

PRINCIPLE 17

Peer pressure is a driving force in the life of a teenager; parents must be aware that it is usually far more important to appease a peer than a parent; yet there will be times when a teen will want to be "reeled in," but not able to convey it in words. It's the parent's job to help the youngster save face with peers by supplying an excuse to resist "bad" decisions.

PRINCIPLE 18

When a child overpowers a parent, both lose. The child who defeats the parent finds him or herself in a terrible paradox. On a conscious level he acquires control and thus an illusion of power; on an unconscious level he becomes terrified that his parents are so weak that even (s)he can defeat them.

PRINCIPLE 19

Inconsistency teaches your child that you cannot be trusted.

PRINCIPLE 20

"Bad places" exist in nearly all relationships because "bad places" exist within all people. In the parent-child relationship, the parent must make sure that all visits to "bad places" are initiated by and limited to the internal world of the child. A child should be protected from having his or her "bad places" compounded by those of the parent.

PRINCIPLE 21

A pure, healthy relationship is one in which two people can be their true selves with no fear, pretense or forced deference; when this occurs between parent and offspring, one of life's greatest joys is experienced. Further, when this relationship does exist, it will likely be repeated later in life within the adult child's new family.

PRINCIPLE 22

By the time a child reaches adolescence, what a parent does is not nearly as important as what has already been done.

PRINCIPLE 23

It is important that parents learn to honor differences between their children, instead of labeling them either good or bad. Children are much more likely to be mentally healthy when they realize that both good and bad elements are a part of themselves and others.

1

INFANCY AND THE PARADOX OF LIFE

Infancy is that one period in your life when "throwing a fit" is the accepted means for getting what you want.

THE FIRST PRINCIPLE OF POWERFUL PARENTING

Both parents must be willing to give love to another and give up the expectation of being loved in return.

A NOTE TO MOTHERS

You'll notice a focus throughout the next few chapters of *Dynamics* on the role of the mother in raising children, especially in the first five years of life. It may seem that the chief responsibility for parenting is the mother's, and that the father is exonerated from his job of parenting. Further, you may get the impression that *Dynamics* is insensitive to the fact that many mothers (single and married) have to work in order to keep their families financially afloat.

But it is my belief that, while the mother is the most important person in the life of any child at any age, the role of the father is critically important as well. He is important to the child in three significant ways.

First, he must be present to support and nurture the mother in mind and spirit; he must be able to continually put his wishes aside to serve the greater good of the mother and the family.

Second, the father should be the first person in the child's life after the mother. Essentially, the father is the first person to whom a child transfers his or her bond with the mother; in other words, the father becomes the second love object in a child's life. If the mother and father work together to achieve these ends, the child will likely grow to be very healthy.

Third, the father becomes part of the parenting couple, each of whom nurtures and disciplines the child as she grows and develops. This aspect of fathering is often overdone, particularly when the mother resorts to "wait until your father gets home," or the father resorts to continual use of anger as a way of controlling behavioral situations.

There is no mistaking it: the mother is, or at least should be, the primary person in a child's life. There is no real way that a father (or some surrogate) can ever become the mother to a child; to think otherwise would deny the reality of the situation. If the mother is somehow replaced by another, a break in attachment between the mother and the child occurs and the child is damaged in some way by this fact; a surrogate can do a good job at compensating for this loss, but he or she cannot become *the* mother. In any event a basic truth seems to be this: the mother (or mother surrogate) is the source of all energy for a child in her first few months and years; this energy becomes materialized as the child herself. The quality of this energy will in large measure determine the quality of the child.

THE GOOD-ENOUGH MOTHER[3]

The good-enough mother is the mother who sacrifices much of her freedom and energies to her infant child. The relationship between mother and child is like that of a sun which orbits a planet. The mother must provide love, attention, food, and other forms of indulgences throughout the infancy period. If this does not happen in a good-enough way, the child can be damaged for life.

Mothering (i.e., good-enough mothering) in infancy involves complete attention given to the gratification of needs (alleviation of tension) presented by the child. These needs are revealed to the mother through the child's crying and angering behaviors. This process of gratification must happen repeatedly throughout infancy (until about the age of one year to fifteen months) in order for the child to learn how to trust and to feel secure in his relationship with the primary caregiver (in most cases, the mother). It is ironic that once infancy ends, the child is expected to quickly unlearn the very behaviors (i.e., crying and angering) that have become part of the core of his existence, especially in the realm of needs gratification.

Assuming good-enough mothering, the paradox of life is this: the infant child, helpless, dependent, empty of knowledge and bereft of awareness, experiences what can be viewed as the most powerful state in

[3]Winnicott, D. W., *Home...*; p. 119.

life. He gets any desire (need) gratified through the simple acts of crying and angering. The adult human being, by the time of middle age, has achieved independence, material wealth, knowledge, self awareness and the illusion of power; yet he must come to terms with the fact that he is totally powerless to control others and further, that he is powerless to stop the inevitable outcome of life.

TRUST AND ANGER

To be an effective parent you must understand the importance of anger in the life of your child. In infancy this means that the parent must become accustomed to meeting the needs of the crying child; grandmother's advice to "let him cry himself to sleep" will not bode well for a child's well being. Ongoing attention to the crying infant, and ongoing gratification of the infant's needs will result in the experience of trust within the child-parent relationship. Eventually this trust will reside within the child herself. It is this trust and the mother's love that brings forth the psychological bond that deepens between the mother and child as the child grows. It is this bond that will provide the foundation for successful relationships in the child's world. If trust is not learned in infancy and a satisfactory bond does not form, the child is likely to become either aggressive or withdrawn, and the child will experience various difficulties with the formation of connections and attachments with others throughout his or her life.

The cycle of trust[4]

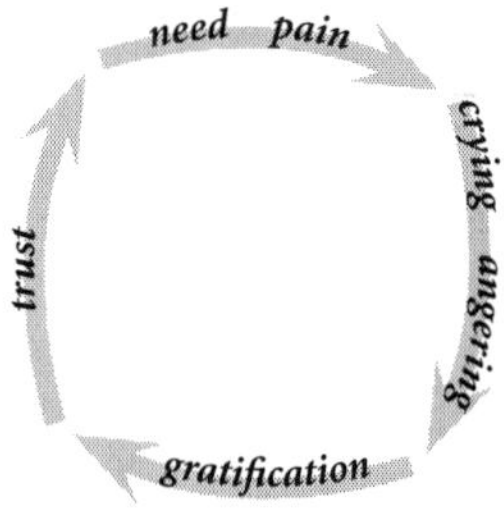

The cycle of trust must be completed during infancy for healthy emotional development. Contrary to what many people think, the mother is *not* the first object of trust for the child in infancy; rather, it is crying and angering that lead to the child's first experiences of trust. The infant learns that when pain arises and she cries or gets angry, the pain will go away; it is not until later, at about two or three months, that the child learns to associate relief with her mother's presence.

---

[4]Cline, *Hope for…*; p. 17.

Parents who do not understand the role of anger in an infant's growth are apt to have problems with their own anger. Sometimes these parents are angry and resentful of the time and energy required to raise a child, and they may begin punishments for "bad behaviors" long before the child would ever be able to understand the reason for them. It should be noted, not all punishments are physical; becoming angry and sullen, and holding on to bad feelings against the child for extended periods of time can result in a great deal of psychological damage that happens prior to the child's ability to remember the event, making it all the more difficult to repair later in life. The parent's worst enemy in the parent-child relationship is anger directed at the child. The harm that can and will be produced by an angry parent can be extensive. *Dynamics* is, in a sense, a workshop for how to deal with anger: yours and your child's.

ATTACHMENT AND LOVE

Parents who are able to tolerate the anger that is displayed by infants, and who are able to selflessly yield to the "demands" of the infant will set the stage for the most important psychological and emotional experience of a person's life: attachment. The psychological attachment that happens inside the mother-child bond is one that grows and strengthens as the mother reinforces the child's ability to trust by way of her presence, availability, and generosity.

Although trust is extremely important, it's not the only ingredient in a successful bond between mother and child. The existence of love in combination with trust produces the most satisfactory outcomes for health and well-being.

Love is a very misunderstood phenomenon among humans. There are as many definitions for love as there are people who ponder it, but suffice it to say that love is that one intangible "substance" that lies at the foundation of the truly healthy person. Children who are raised in loving, non-affluent families are invariably healthier and better satisfied with their lives than children who are raised in more affluent families but with less contact with loving parents. The ills of having "too much" are best understood by those who have had "too much" and have had to work their way through the misery of expecting life to be easy and accommodating.

Attachment is a result of a loving and trusting interaction between mother and child on a routine basis in a consistent manner. A sense of well-being is transferred to the infant child by way of the mother's voice, touch, eye contact, demeanor, attitude, and overall disposition. These attributes of the mother cannot be "faked" nor learned in a classroom or book; they must be already present and, if not, they must be acquired through the maturation that occurs by way of social discourse, interpersonal tension, self examination and reconciliation (with self and others).

The process of attachment and its effects upon the developing human being cannot be emphasized greatly enough. Attachment is the absolute foundation for the structure that will eventually become a healthy, well adjusted, secure adult person. Many things can happen to a person throughout a lifetime, some of them traumatic or heartbreaking, but the well-attached person (even from a dysfunctional family) will be able to rise above these hardships and go on to survive and thrive; the unattached person most often will not. If it were not for the processes of attachment, trust, and love, human beings would be bereft of compassion; mere animals with magnificent intelligence, but no heart.

THE DILEMMA: ANGRY ATTACHMENTS

PRINCIPLE 2

> *Mothers and fathers need to work in concert together for the benefit of their children. When they do not, children can easily become weapons in their fight against one another.*

It's important to explore the issue of anger within the parent, to examine and ultimately understand it; the power of anger to disrupt and negatively influence the quality of the child-mother bond is enormous.

Parents who are quick to anger are often people who have felt powerless in their interpersonal relationships for most of their lives. Men who were dominated by their fathers, scorned by their mothers, or rejected by their siblings often find themselves struggling for selfworth, and in this struggle they often resort to attempts to gain power (i.e., by angering) over their wives and children. It is the same for women who competed with their mothers for their father's love, who were rejected by father, or were dominated by their mother's will. They, too, struggle for power in their relationships with their husbands and their children.

The dynamic of power for women and men can be dramatically different. One stereotype is well known: Men are overtly controlling and often try to get their way by expressing anger to control things. Women tend to yield to this bid for power (i.e., anger) in the short-term, but internalize a great deal of their own anger in the form of resentment, and will strive to gain power in the family through covert means. Many times this dynamic is manifest in the gradual withdrawal of love from the husband while over-compensating for this loss by showering a greater abundance of love onto her children.

On the surface this would appear to be a good thing for infants and small children, but the positive psychological energy of the system is siphoned away from the father, and is then replaced with negative energy within both parents toward one another. Often, the mother will form an "alliance" with the children that will result in too much power over the authority of the father, and the mother will later have to pay the price of seeing the children's behaviors deteriorate; many times she will find herself with difficult children and no partner to whom she can turn.

It is important for every father to realize that the mother must rightfully dedicate what seems to be an inordinate amount of time and energy to the infant child, and that he may suffer an emotional loss of his wife after the first child is born. This, very naturally, reinforces any feelings of inadequacy already held by the father, and creates a withdrawal of positive emotional energy from the mother (the mirror image of what happens with mother as outlined above) which results in resentments (albeit suppressed) that can be directed by the father toward his children.

These dynamics leave the parenting partners divided and both are eventually rendered ineffective for maintaining authority over the developing children. When this occurs, the rift between the mother and father only widens and each attempts to blame the other for the problems in the family. At this point, some couples require copious amounts of marital intervention and parenting education, or they will fall into divorce. It should be noted that staying married for the sake of the children is not nearly as good for a family as is improving the quality of the marriage for the same reason.

A SOLUTION

When a couple decides upon marriage, it's time to start discussing the matter of children. Do they want children? How many will they want? How many do they think they'll be able to afford? This is when a couple should start talking about their relationship. This is when they should be learning to talk openly about each other's traits and foibles. They should take a close look at their own parents and their families of origin, and discuss potential strengths and weaknesses in their union.

It is imperative that the future mother be aware that she will lose most of the freedoms she may once have enjoyed, and if she will be a working mother, she must realize that her workload will increase dramatically. The future father needs to come to terms with the fact that his wife will have less and less time for him. He must learn to accept his wife's efforts to delegate many household and childcare responsibilities to him, and to accept these responsibilities without complaint. The father must remember that when his wife becomes a mother she is in a whole new world, and the focus of the marriage will shift greatly. The father must learn to handle his wife's moods and preoccupation with mothering; the mother must learn to find new ways to let her husband know that she is still interested in him. The couple should discuss specific tasks such as night feedings, formula preparation, grocery shopping, housekeeping, bill paying, diaper changing, "babysitting," child care and many others so that they can agree with what needs to be done before they get started. They should consult the very thorough recommendations given by Dr. Spock in his books to learn about the "nuts and bolts" details of childrearing.

Potential parents should do these things in an effort to examine their attitudes about parenting and how their differences might affect how they will raise their children, as well as how their children might be affected by their differences. Although some couples may find these attempts at communication very difficult, and may in some cases decide to end the relationship, it will be far better for the child not yet born that prospective partners (and thus, future parents) work to determine a healthy course for their lives.

These very simple solutions are easy to pose and easy to recommend prior to a child's arrival, but are extremely difficult to execute after the child is born. The best way to address any concerns of marital differences and marital agreements is with the help of a skilled counselor or clergyperson.

CONCLUSION

Effective parenting in infancy is the ongoing application of the mother's love to the developing infant. It is virtually impossible to raise a damaged child in a loving and emotionally balanced environment. When patience, love, and acceptance are accorded to each mate by the other (especially from the husband to the wife), raising a family is a true joy; on the other hand when selfishness, irritability, impatience, and hostility are applied to the family experience, pure misery results for all (especially the children). Both parents are pivotal for the development of a strong family; the mother must be willing to devote the vast majority of her energies to the baby, and the father must be able to tolerate the emotional loss of his spouse while dedicating his energies to the care and nurturance of his wife and children.

Throughout *Dynamics* you'll find questions at the end of each chapter which give you a chance to pause and reflect on the issues discussed and how you experienced them. These questions may be difficult, and may lead to some guilt and regret; these are natural feelings and natural responses for parents learning that no parent is the perfect parent.

Worksheet

WHAT ABOUT YOUR CHILD'S INFANCY?

1. List no less than five needs experienced by any baby.

2. What is a major potential negative outcome of premature births, or colicky babies?

3. What are your thoughts on working mothers and leaving children in professional daycare for prolonged periods of the day?

4. If given the chance, would you prefer to have your child with the same private sitter each day or use a daycare facility?

5. Consider the following:
   - Did you breast feed or bottle feed?
   - Did your child make good eye contact with you while feeding?
   - Did you readily attend to you child when he or she cried during the day?
   - Did you readily and "joyfully" attend to your child when he or she cried in the night?
   - Did you wait for your baby to cry, or did you try to anticipate his or her needs in advance?
   - Was your baby colicky? How did you handle this physically? emotionally?
   - Did you spend ample time with your baby while awake, or did you leave him alone in a crib or playpen?
   - How active was dad in the parenting of your infant child?
   - What was your underlying feeling tone regarding your child(ren)? Depressed, despondent, worried, anxious, relaxed; nervous, angry, irritated, embarrassed?
   - Why did you have your baby? What effect do you think your reason might have on the child's life in the long-term?
6. After reviewing these questions, what quality of trust would you assign to the results of your efforts to be a good-enough mother for your baby? Circle a number on the graph below.

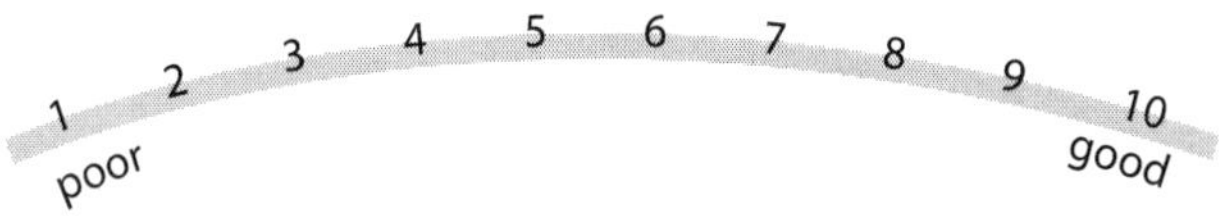

7. How did you and you husband decide upon division of labor after your first child was born? Did you plan or did you "make it up as you went along?" How did it work out?

2

SEPARATION: TODDLERHOOD AND THE TYRANNICAL CHILD

Anything goes when there is no guilt.
Be glad toddlers are little.

Imagine for a moment what it must be like to be a king or queen who has been deposed from power; what it must be like to be a prince one day and a pauper the next. This is how it is for a child to move from infancy to toddlerhood. In chapter one, we saw the infant as the center of the universe for the mother. Now the toddler must now learn to allow the mother to the be the center of his world. More often than not, this transition is not an easy thing to accept.

It is important that parents realize that the terrible two's is a concept that was coined by tired and frustrated parents; after all, the life of the young toddler is a life of joy and wonderment interspersed with periods of volcanic activity. There is no guilt in the toddler child, and where there is no guilt there is total emotional and behavioral freedom.

There are various developmental tasks of toddlerhood (talking, self-feeding, toilet training, walking, running, and more) that are very important to healthy development; however, when considering emotional development, two stand above all the rest: separation from mother (both physical and emotional), and conscience development (acquiring the ability to feel guilt).

The successful accomplishment of these two processes is the key to raising healthy children.

PRINCIPLE 3

Parents control the environment and set the limits of the child's freedom. The earlier a parent learns the art of being powerless over a child, the easier the job of parenting.

TODDLER-PROOFING

A parent should know from very early in a child's life that only he has the power to control his behavior. It is an illusion that parents actually do things that control children. As a parent, you must accept that you are in a position only to create a world for your child that is carefully designed to provide experiences that are as close to "real life" as possible. You have to learn to let go of trying to control the child and trust that she will learn many of life's lessons independent of the parent's influence. The world is new for each child, and each learns according to her talents, strengths, and abilities.

The process of designing the child's world begins in toddlerhood with the notion of "toddler-proofing" the home. When your home has been toddler-proofed, your child is free to roam at his discretion. Toddlers fall, bump their heads, write on walls, tear up magazines, and on and on, but from each hurtful experience they learn a lesson. Toddler-proofing limits the amount of damage that the child can experience and perpetrate upon themselves and the home.

Toddler-proofing a home is not only important for the safety of the child and home, but it is also important for the psychological and emotional development of the growing child. The more freedom afforded a toddler, the greater the amount of personal growth that can take place away from the mother (and/or father). Freedom gives way to separation.

SEPARATION

PRINCIPLE 4

The word No *is far and away the single most important word in your child's vocabulary. Its importance is equally divided between his ability to both give and receive it.*

It is extremely difficult for a child to develop a separate identity unless he is allowed to pull away from the mother so that the he experiences life on his own terms. Often, this is not an easy task for either child or parent. After all, toddlerhood is a time of learning to give up power, and no one really wants to do that. Separating is not easy for the child because of anger and frustration; it is not easy for the parent due to the child's behaviors; yet parents should know and understand that a child's negative reactions to parental limits are normal.

Separation is one of three processes in toddlerhood that essentially distances and defines the child in relationship to the mother and others: the other two processes are individuation, and differentiation.[5] It should be noted that these three processes occur consecutively with some overlap during the first three years.

Toddlers have a language for the processes of identity formation. It is a very simple, yet effective language that many adults will experience as negative and undesirable.

THE LANGUAGE OF SEPARATION

The word that toddlers use to separate from others is *No;* of all the words available to a child, *No* is likely to be the most important. It is *No* that says "I am not willing"; it is *No* that says "I am apart from you." Very often children who attempt to say *No* to their parents are considered defiant and therefore "bad." The parent will often attempt to teach the child that *No* is simply not an option by coercing or guilting the child to comply with parental requests. This will naturally lead to an argument in which there will be anger and hurt feelings on both sides. However, the responsible parent realizes that *No* is valuable to a child; the responsible parent will exercise patience and wisdom in response to a child's efforts to separate from the parent's will and authority. The responsible parent will sometimes allow the child to have his way in various situations, only to come back to the child on the very same issue in the future. Successful separation results in a person who is able to stand apart from the rest of the world and make decisions within herself; decisions that are reflective of effective and acceptable means for meeting one's needs.

For example, Johnny is asked to pick up his shoes from the living room floor. He responds by saying *No.* The parent asks Johnny again and Johnny still says *No.* The parent then moves past this act of defiance and appears to forget it. A little later, Johnny wants ice cream as his treat after dinner. The parent simply says: "You may have your ice cream after you've put your shoes away." If Johnny puts his shoes away, he'll get his treat; if he doesn't,he won't.

---

[5]Mahler, M., *Psychological Birth...*; p. 52.

Either way, trust is enforced between the parent and the child, while the child is permitted to make his decision. (See *Win/Win Parenting*, page 156.)

In this example the child is allowed to say *No*, but is also given the freedom to eventually learn that by choosing to do what he is asked (i.e., being compliant), he may be able to avoid being inconvenienced. All of this is learned behaviorally and accomplished without anger, coercion, or manipulating the child. All done by controlling the environment (Principle 3).

THE LANGUAGE OF INDIVIDUATION

Simply put, individuation is the process that produces a child who knows he is an individual in his world. The words for this process are I, me, and mine. When a child starts to use these words she is telling the world "I am here; reckon with me." Successful individuation produces a person who is able to stand on her own two feet and take a stand to represent herself to those around her. There is an added dimension to the word mine, in that mine implies ownership and belonging. The child who says "my house," "my mommy," "my chair," etcetera, is learning that she is connected to her world and she is claiming her portion of it.

THE LANGUAGE OF DIFFERENTIATION

Differentiation is the process that yields the child's understanding that he is different from everybody else, and that everybody else is different from one another. Words such as he, his, she, her, hers, they, them, and theirs demonstrate that the child is able to discern himself from the others in the world. These words also indicate that the child is learning to distinguish others in the world, one from another.

SEPARATION ANXIETY

PRINCIPLE **5**

> *Become the most important person in your child's life, but do this because he is the most important person in yours.*

* * *

> *Little Bo Peep lost her sheep and didn't know where to find them; She left them alone and they came home, wagging their tails behind them.*
>
> – *Nursery Rhyme*

This stage of development occurs around nine months, before the child is old enough to verbalize feelings; yet it is clear from examination of the child's behavior that separation is often a distressful process. However, it is important to keep in mind that it should be more distressful for the child than for the parent. It is important that mothers realize that the discomfort suffered by a child during this stage is a natural part of human growth and that the child will actually develop a stronger and more intimate attachment to the mother if handled properly.

Parents, especially mothers, need to know that separation anxiety results from the fact that a child's mind and body are rapidly developing. The child is becoming aware of her environment and is responding to tension within the bond with mother; therefore, separation anxiety is a signal to the mother that her infant is well-bonded and that this bond is being tested. If the child fails to display separation anxiety, it is likely that the bond with mother is tentative, loose, or poorly formed. The child doesn't show much distress because the loss is not felt as keenly as with a well-bonded child. Such children are said to be detached. On the other hand, some mothers create a bond that is too close (enmeshed); such children are inconsolable when separated from mother. This is often a result of a mother who fears separation in her own right and transfers her own heightened separation anxiety onto her child. The child experiences mother's anxiety as a reinforcement of her own anxiety, and thereby can be emotionally calm only in the mother's presence. These children will exhibit behaviors upon separation that the anxious mother will see as viable reasons to remain available for the child (thus promoting ever more clinging behaviors...see example in *hostile-dependency* pp. 102 -104).

RAPPROCHEMENT (REUNION)[6]

As noted earlier, toddlerhood is the process in which the world focus shifts for the infant child. No longer the center of the universe, the child must learn to rely and depend on mother to be that center. Separation anxiety is one element of the developmental process that helps put the mother at the center of the system (Principle 5). Mother must know that there is nothing wrong with a child who cries when separated and she must refrain from negative attitudes about the process (particularly in the forms of feeling sorry for, or angry at, her child). Also, it is important that mother face the separation process with confidence (trust) that the child can and will successfully overcome the momentary anguish of separation from the

[6]Mahler, ibid.

mother. And finally, it is extremely important that when reunited, mother should always be happy to see baby (even when baby is not happy to see her).

Separation anxiety leads to "coming back" behaviors so that when the child gets too far away from the mother, he or she will "come back" and seek refuge within mother's love once again. This process of coming back is labeled "rapprochement," French for reunion and reconciliation (pronounced rä-prôsh-mä). This process is of the utmost importance for the formation of conscience (as will be pointed out in the following chapter).

If separation anxiety issues are not successfully resolved by the end of toddlerhood, the child will likely exhibit various forms of enmeshed behaviors throughout childhood (and beyond). The enmeshment behaviors that arise as a result of poor resolution of separation anxiety issues tend to be of three kinds: frightened-clingy, oppositional-defiant, and hostile-dependent.

What will follow will be brief descriptions of each style of functioning (or "dysfunctioning," as the case may be); please refer to Chapter 7 for more detailed examinations of each.

The frightened-clingy child is the child who simply has a great deal of difficulty with mother's absence. Many rationalizations and excuses are offered for children stuck in this manner of relating. It is important for parents to realize that there is nothing really the matter with the frightened-clingy child except for the parent's insistence that the child is somehow "defective" and requires the parent's presence in order to survive the rigors of the child's existence (see Chapter 7 pg. 99 for more details about the frightened-clingy child).

The oppositional-defiant child is often a child who is struggling with a separation anxiety problem but can do so only by becoming a disciplinary problem for the parents. These children become "problem children" in that parents and other authority figures are not able to view the child's defiance and oppositionalism as as acts of self-determination, but are instead seen to be "bad" or problematic. It is of the utmost importance that adults learn to deal with oppositional-defiant children in a manner that avoids conflict and head-to-head confrontations (see Chapter 7, pg. 101 for a more detailed description and resolution of the oppositional-defiant child).

The hostile-dependent child is a blended variation of the two previous styles. She will remain dependent upon her parents, but will treat them with disdain in the process. The hostile-dependent person often creates situations that appear intractable to both the child and the parents. When the parents (often without having to be asked) step in to rescue the child, she is very happy to accept the help, only to quickly resume a negative relational experience for both the parent and the offspring, neither of whom are able to pull out of the enmeshment; the offspring, because it is just too easy to accept the largess of the parent, and the parent due to the guilt and feelings of anxiety that the offspring can't live without the parent (see Chapter 7, page 101 for information about the hostile-dependent style of parent-child interaction).

LIMITS AND BOUNDARIES

PRINCIPLE 6

A parent must be confident and able to tolerate negative feelings from a child. An attitude of confidence and assurance must be transmitted to the child, especially from toddlerhood on. Confident parenting will yield confident children.

Two keys to successful separation, individuation, and differentiation are limits and boundaries, two words that are often used interchangeably with one another. However, they are not the same, and it is important to understand the difference between the two. A limit is some restriction that is placed upon a child by a parent. Examples of limits might be:

- a taboo on wall-writing
- no sweets until after dinner
- bedtimes
- television shows
- foods types
- curfews

Limits are usually maintained by way of the execution of authority.

A boundary, on the other hand, is a behavior or set of behaviors that puts a clear distance between two people. Examples of boundaries are things such as:

- doors and knocking on them to gain entrance
- respecting privacy
- refusing a child admittance to a purse of wallet
- giving and taking *No* for an answer (both parents and children)
- keeping hands to self
- refraining from taking more than one's share
- saying *No* to sex on a date
- refusing to allow another to copy one's work
- refusing to accept abusive behaviors from another

Boundaries are more related to the understanding of human dignity and personal sovereignty rather than the exercise of parental authority. Limits and boundaries can be taught to a child on a daily basis when a parent understands and exercises their importance.

Parents can do things such as:

- respect privacy
- allow a child to say *No* in harmless or non-disciplinary situations
- accept that a child won't always be disposed to grant a "favor"
- accept that a child can and will "speak her mind."
- allow for a child to choose clothes (and daily outfits)
- permit the child to roam and wander (in controlled situations)

Many, many people (children and adults alike) find that limits and boundaries are extremely difficult to set and maintain because of the lack of acceptance of such by others.

Throughout their lives they have become conditioned to expect negativity, criticism, and anger whenever attempts are made to impose them. The results of failed attempts at applying limits and boundaries are emotional and behavioral problems such as overeating, alcoholism, drug addiction, codependency, depression, anxiety, and rage. Successful application of limits and boundaries results in a person who is respectful of others, self-disciplined, relatively happy, and is emotionally well-balanced within a well-defined character.

A FINAL WORD ABOUT SEPARATION

When the processes of separation, individuation, and differentiation are well-executed in toddlerhood, the child will likely develop a strong sense of identity and self-determination, and will be able to feel okay about herself when either being challenged by, or challenging, another. However, when these processes are compromised, the child will likely either become angry and defiant or anxious and clingy. The primary solution to problems involving separation in toddlerhood is for parents to acquire confidence in their efforts to set and maintain limits and boundaries with their children. (*Time-out,* page 137, and *Win/Win Parenting,* page 156, offer tools for increasing parental confidence.)

Worksheet

SEPARATION

1. Thinking about your child (toddler and up), how do you remember:

    - Leaving her in her crib for a nap?

    - Dropping him off at the sitter's?

    - Briefly leaving him a room alone while you attended to another task or person?

    - While you were watching a TV program or reading a book?

2. List the vocabulary of

    - Separation

    - Individuation

    - Differentiation

3. What do you remember about your child learning the separation words?

    - Separation

    - Individuation

    - Differentiation

4. How did (does) your child take *No* for an answer in toddlerhood?

5. How did (do) you handle your child's manner for dealing with *No?*

6. How does your child take *No* for an answer now? Are you okay with this? If not, what do you think went wrong? What might you do to correct things?

7. Do you see your relationship with your child as well-defined and well-centered? anxious-clingy? detached? Why?

8. How do you feel regarding your answer to the previous question?

9. How do you see your child's identity and sense of self?
   - Does she mix well with other children? Is she shy? Aggressive?
   - Is he comfortable playing and/or being alone?
   - Does she make good eye contact with you? How about with others?
   - Is he able to stand his ground with others without fighting or running away?

3

Conscience

PRINCIPLE 7

Anger is the fire that tempers character; this anger should come from the child, not the parent.

At about 42 months of age (give or take a few months), the developing child should display the elements of an active conscience. These elements are revealed in behaviors such as:

- traits of compassion and care for others
- sorrow over the suffering of another (sometimes an injured animal)
- empathy
- concern for someone who is ill or incapacitated
- sadness and regret for hurtful behaviors directed at another
- movement away from laughing and poking fun at another's misfortune

The conscionable child should begin to display visible guilt (eyes and head down in an attitude of shame) and should also show some propensity for making "good" choices (knowing right from wrong).

THE INGREDIENTS OF CONSCIENCE DEVELOPMENT:
A PSYCHOLOGICAL DYNAMIC PERSPECTIVE

The first ingredient: Anger

The first and most visible ingredient in conscience development is the child's anger. As has been noted earlier, toddlerhood is often punctuated by recurrent temper losses on the part of the child, and as was further noted, this is how it should be. It is up to the parent to realize that temper losses in toddlerhood are not "bad," and it is important to know that when a child loses his temper, this does not mean that the child is "bad." Many people will condemn or criticize a child for having tantrums, and will label him as a "cry baby," "spoiled brat," or "little tyrant." Effective, healthy parents know that tantrums are part of normal development and they also know that chastising a child for crying (and in doing so, chastising them for being normal) is one of the surest ways to inflict deep emotional wounds.

Consider Daphne, a three year old toddler, and her mother:

> Daphne and her mother are about to go through the checkout at the supermarket. Mother is pushing a cart loaded with groceries when the little girl sees her favorite candy on the rack at the checkout aisle. Daphne asks mother if she may have the candy. Mother says *No.* When Daphne asks why, the mother tells her it's because she has not yet had her lunch. Daphne starts to argue and gets louder in her efforts to obtain the candy bar. The mother tells her that she will not buy her the candy, but it is okay for her to cry.

Daphne's anger is the fire that is beginning to warm the cauldron of the mother-child relationship. When she gets angry at her mother, she is experiencing a sort of temporary hatred for her mother which can sometimes go very deep. If mother responds with her own fear, anger, and/or guilt, Daphne will learn two significantly different and opposing lessons about relating to her mother. First, when mother gets angry or irritated at her, she learns that she herself feels badly; second, she learns that she has power over her mother's emotions in that she is able to get mother "rattled." However, if mother remains calm and steady, and handles Daphne's anger with compassion and coolness, Daphne will experience her mother as firm and immovable. This will result in a loss of power for Daphne, but she will learn that her world is stable, and she will learn that she must adapt to the ways of the external world.

This loss of power will lead to either submission or escalation. If

Daphne were to submit at this point in the exchange, mother would respond by acknowledging and appreciating Daphne for doing so. If, on the other hand, Daphne escalates her efforts to sway her mother, mother will have to hold firm in her limit and maintain her sense of steadiness in the situation, as illustrated in the sections that follow.

HATRED AND "DEATH TO THE PARENT"

In the early going of a child's life or in the initial stages of changes made in a child's life (e.g., , during a move, divorce, or when implementing therapy or counseling), the child will often escalate his behaviors in an effort to gain power and return to familiar ground in the child-parent relationship. Many times a child will resort to such things as "I hate you," or "I wish you were dead"; these words are, more or less, the child's last ditch effort to "get to the parent."

Time and again, parents will consider the words "I hate you" and "I wish you were dead" to be on a par with profanity and total disrespect; when a parent reacts to such words with strong emotion and ineffective anger, the child learns that these words have the power to cause a reaction in the parent. Yet, if the parent succeeds in eradicating these displays of by punishing the child (a form of vindictive and controlling anger), the child suffers a tremendous defeat and at the same time is unable to express the strong emotions that accompany this kind of defeat. Both situations represent a loss of power for both the child and/or the parent, and can be avoided through the use of simple acts of tolerance on the part of the parent for a child's anger in difficult situations. (Please note, contrary to what some parents might think, tolerance for a child's anger is not the same as "letting the child get way with murder.")

PRINCIPLE 8

> *In family situations, most people don't behave much differently than they feel. This is especially true for children. Forcing a child to "behave" when she feels otherwise, teaches her to avoid feeling as a way to escape punishment. As an adult she will likely have great difficulty with future family situations.*

The fact is, many children experience strong emotions on a regular basis and need to find words to express them; when denied the ability to do so, they will learn to avoid strong feelings by sublimating (ignoring) and/or denying them. When feelings are sublimated and/or denied, they may appear to be absent and the child may appear to be obedient and compliant, but these negative feelings are likely to remain active for motivating a child's future behaviors, particularly when the child is out of the parent's sphere of influence. Imagine young Daphne in our story being severely punished by her mother for crying. Mother would have had to escalate her own anger to muster the power to "force" Daphne to stop behaving "badly." Daphne would have had to comply out of fear for her physical safety. Chances are Daphne might eventually have to learn to be a "good little girl" when in her mother's presence; then later "get even" by acting-out when mother's not looking.

Parents of small children must recognize that it is natural and understandable for children (unlike adults) to try to hurt others with strong words to rid themselves of the very "bad" feelings that exist within. Parents must learn to employ a process that teaches children the importance of taming such emotions throughout the maturation process. Parents need remember that, for a child to learn to behave well, especially when wanting to do otherwise, a process of adaptation must be employed rather than the use of a series of punishments in early childhood.

Natural hatred (as opposed to the hatred resulting from indoctrination) is an ongoing occurrence for the immature, developing child. This type of hatred is a by-product of mixing anger and shame which will result in a deep inner pain; the child will naturally lash out at the person or persons he believes caused it (i.e., resort to blaming behaviors).

Hatred is a very base and primal feeling state, and it must be handled in the same way as the child's anger (i.e., with parental restraint and compassion). Parents must learn to take away the power of hatred by remaining calm within themselves and treating it as a form of self-expression. Parents must trust that as they apply compassion and containment to the child's anger and hatred, the child will grow and mature. As a child matures within an environment of compassionate containment, the child's expressions of hatred and rage will diminish in frequency and intensity.

The second ingredient: Shame

PRINCIPLE 9

> *There is never any need to intentionally shame a child; life is a harsh taskmaster and will yield numerous failures; rest assured, there will be more than enough shame along the way for a child to "learn his lesson."*

The second ingredient for conscience development is the young child's experience of shame. This shame is not yet the awareness of guilt, but rather a more pure feeling that hurts the child from the inside out.

Shame is one of the basic components of a person's inner emotional world. It is a natural feeling that emerges when a person perceives that he or she has failed in some way. The roots of shame can be traced back to toddlerhood.

Toddlers are slowly becoming aware of themselves. They are learning through separation that they are distinct beings who must interact with their world as part of being alive. The advent of toddlerhood brings forth an awareness of self and with this, an awakening to the experiences of success and failure. When a child experiences success, he feels good, almost joyful; when the child experiences failure, he experiences the feeling of shame; a very uncomfortable, painful, and unwanted state of being.

Shame hurts.

Let's revisit Daphne and her mother.

> Daphne's mother is now in the midst of emptying her cart onto the conveyor. Daphne is still crying and trying to change her mother's mind about the candy bar. Daphne has told her mother that she is a mean mommy, that mommy doesn't love her anymore, because if she did she would get the candy for her, and now she doesn't love mommy anymore.
>
> Mom continues to complete her purchase. Her face is red; it is clear that she is feeling something, yet she remains committed to the task at hand: getting out of the store.

It must be remembered that toddlers are only a few months past infancy, and as such, toddlers will handle their hurt feelings in much the same way as they handled them in infancy: they will cry, and if crying doesn't work, they will get angry. When toddlers get angry they are absolutely devoid of any restraints and will do and say anything to get what they want.

As was noted in the previous section, angry toddlers are often looked upon with disdain and scorn whenever they act out their negative feelings. The reason for this is that most people see childhood anger as bad; however, in order for a healthy conscience to develop, a change in perspective is needed for parents of toddler children.

A SHAME-BASED INTERPRETATION: TWO POINTS OF VIEW

The child's perspective

In the above example, Daphne is experiencing shame. This shame is generated on two levels. First, she feels the immediate shame of thinking that her mother doesn't love her anymore because she won't indulge her. Shame hurts; Daphne cries as a result.

Second, Daphne is experiencing failure. The candy bar is the object of her desire; she wants it. Not getting it is a defeat. When a child (or any person for that matter) feels defeated, a failure is perceived, and shame results. Shame hurts; Daphne cries as a result.

Many parents are familiar with the childhood taunt, "if you loved me, you'd get it for me." This attempt to manipulate the parent is born in the feeling that withheld gratification is akin to the withdrawal of love. When a child perceives that love has been withdrawn, she will feel unworthy; when she feels unworthy, she will experience the feeling of shame.

The mother's perspective

Mother is also experiencing shame. While standing in the checkout line, she feels the shame of embarrassment due to the misbehavior of her child. Her efforts to refute her daughter's request may likely have resulted from her thoughts that others will think that she is spoiling her child if she gives in to her (a shame-based thought). To make matters worse, when Daphne begins to cry, mother fears that everyone in the store is now looking at her and judging her for being a "bad" parent. At this point, mother is clearly experiencing shame, but this mother is not giving in to her feelings and is determined to move ahead in spite of her daughter's protests.

The third ingredient: Love and stability

A parent's adherence to unwavering love and understanding of the toddler's inner struggles is the next step toward the child's conscience formation. Many parents, when addressed with the notion that it is important to be calm with a crying child will ask, "Well then, what am I supposed to do, give in to these tantrums? Should I let the child have her way?"

The answer is a resounding *No.*

When *No* is the answer given by a parent, it is likely (as shown above) that the child will respond with crying and angering. If this crying and angering gets out of control, the parent will have to do something to contain the situation and respond to the disciplinary needs of the child.

Let's return to Daphne and her mother at the market.

> Throughout the mêlée at the checkout counter, Daphne's mother maintains her stance that she cannot have the candy bar. Mother also controls and maintains her own temper. She is visibly upset by her daughter's escalating protests, but nonetheless she does not give in to her desire to become angry at and punish Daphne with either threats or physical punishments. Also, it should be noted that Daphne's mother did not yield to the temptation to give into Daphne's demands and let her have the candy bar. Mother finishes her shopping and heads for the car with Daphne in tow.

It should now be apparent that there is clearly a shame element to refusals given by a mother to her child. If the mother is able to contain her own feelings, and if she is able to see the child's behavior as a reflection of the child's inner feelings, then she can act in a way to keep things from worsening. Daphne's act of raging is the emotional equivalent of separating and distancing from her mother; in other words, her anger creates a wall that does not allow her to feel love for her mother (this emotionally separates Daphne from her mother). It is this separation from the mother (and the feeling of diminished love) that permits the child to continue to rage in an effort to get what she wants.

Many times children will stop raging when the parent changes the context of the situation by simply moving on to another venue; doing this creates *physical separation*, initiated by mother, that may override the *emotional separation* (the distance created by the child). It is likely that as soon as Daphne's mother begins to head for the parking lot, Daphne will change her focus from obtaining the candy bar to reconnecting with her mother who is now moving away from her. Often this shift of focus, in and of itself, will be enough to bring the child to her senses, and will thus bring the child in contact with her own desire to reconnect with her mother. When Daphne changes her focus from the candy to the mother, she adopts the new goal of reconnecting with her mother. All mother needs do at this point would be to accept the daughter back into her loving orbit and move on; Daphne then experiences this reconnection with mother as a success and thus a satisfying (non-shameful) experience.

Be careful with this. The process of "moving away" should not be used as a threat to control the child, but should, instead, be a genuine, yet moderated movement away from the child. Often, a parental move of just a few steps will result in a change of the child's focus (as long as the parent stands firm and waits for the child to close the gap).

The fourth ingredient: Containment

The formation of a healthy conscience requires that parents allow children to expel anger, and then allow them to reconnect (reconsider rapprochement of Chapter 2). In those cases where a parent's feelings interfere with the child's reconnection with the parent, the child will remain distant and will learn to hold on to darker feelings, and not permit herself to give in to the parent's love. This refusal to give in is not merely a rejection of the parent's authority. Rather, this refusal is a conscious effort to refute a parent's efforts to gain control, coupled with the unconscious unwillingness of the child to feel and experience the mixture of love and hurt that is hidden beneath the rage. Parents must learn to reach the child's inner love and hurt while avoiding the use of coercion when providing discipline and containment. This is accomplished by learning to physically restrain them in an attitude of loving firmness and confidence.

Let's return to Daphne and her mother once again.

> Daphne was in a particularly foul mood that day and did not let go of her anger when mother moved toward the parking lot. Mother found herself struggling with transferring groceries to the car and dealing with Daphne's very visible anger. She finally managed to load the groceries, which proved to be a much easier task than getting Daphne secured in her car seat. Mother drove home and Daphne continued to wail that she wanted candy and that she hated her mother for not getting it for her.
>
> By the time they arrived at home, Daphne's mother was beside herself. She was clearly upset that Daphne had escalated her behavior to such proportions. She left Daphne strapped in her car seat until she got the frozen foods put away. Then, she took a few moments to slow down, breathe, and think as she

> returned to her situation with Daphne.
>
> She got back out to the car, undid Daphne's restraints, and against Daphne's protestations, carried her into her room. Once there, mother held Daphne very securely in her arms. Daphne flailed and screamed and threatened all manner of evil against her mother; mother assured her that it was okay to be angry, but that she was not going to let her go until she was calm.
>
> Daphne raged about ten minutes more. Throughout, mother held her and fended off Daphne's every attempt to inflict pain upon her; mother continually repeated that it was okay to be mad and that she loved her, but that she was not going to let go until Daphne was calm.
>
> All of the sudden, as though struck by a bolt, Daphne started to sob. She moved toward her mother, hugging her, saying she was sorry for being so bad. Mother hugged her in return, assuring her that she was a good girl and that getting mad is something that happens to children all the time; together the two of them cried, mother for a few seconds, Daphne for a few minutes.
>
> And then it was over; mother and daughter were reunited. They moved to the kitchen where Daphne very cheerfully helped her mom put away the groceries. Daphne maintained this attitude of cooperation for the next several days.

This finale to Daphne's trip to the store clearly illustrates what is meant by containment. Mother found herself in a position where she had no other choice but to physically restrain and contain her child. In many other families, in similar situations, another parent might have been tempted to spank or punish a child like Daphne for displaying and acting-out unwanted and unacceptable behaviors; to do so in a situation as described here would be extremely harmful to the child-parent relationship.

Many parents ask, "When should I restrain my child?" In most situations, when a parent desires to strike at or punish a child it is time for the parent to step back and consider less hostile alternatives. Often, it is at this point that the parent can choose to exercise a holding or restraint, and by doing so, return control of the situation to the parent, all the while allowing for the continued expression of rage on the part of the child.

Containment and holding are especially effective when a child is able to expel anger without parental reprisals. There comes a point when the child's anger has been fully expended and a void is left in its wake. This absence of anger now makes it possible for the child to experience the very deep pain of having been emotionally separated from the mother. The child will then move back toward the mother, usually in an attitude of sadness, remorse and regret; this reunion takes place from the child toward the mother and rapprochement (reunion and reconciliation) is achieved.

It should be noted that the primary direction of energy of rapprochement is from the child toward the parent (mother in early toddlerhood; father later); the parent must hold steady and receive the child in an attitude of love. It is the parent's love that promotes forgiveness and acceptance of the now-softened child. The parent can then hold the child for a while (reassuring her that she is okay and that it is okay for her to lose her temper) and finally move on. When consistently repeated, the end result is a child who, surprisingly enough, rages less, is healthier, happier, and far more considerate of the feelings of others.

Many parents are reluctant to employ any method in which a child's negative behaviors are not immediately addressed and eliminated on the grounds that allowing a child to be angry and "disrespectful" will only promote such behaviors in the future. Study and experience have shown that whenever children are punished for expressing powerful emotions, the emotional energy will be internalized and will emerge later, often at an inopportune time or place. It is of the utmost importance that parents come to terms with the "process" nature of parenting and the notion that whatever a parent does in any particular moment will become part of the process from which the child develops. Anger begets anger, and when anger is used as a principle part of a parent's approach, the child will likely grow into either an angry or a frightened person, both child and parent will be likely to be affected with shame, self doubt, and negativity.

Thus, it is reasonable and logical to conclude that when temperance and restraint are employed as the underpinning for a parent's efforts at discipline, the resulting person will be one who eventually learns temperance and restraint. Resolving the experiences of anger and rage within a child is much like toilet training: back off from pressuring him and he will eventually get tired of the hassle of wearing diapers and will quit on his own; make a big deal out of anger and the child will learn the power of oppositionalism and resistance, and then continue the battle throughout his development.

A FEW MORE WORDS ABOUT CONTAINMENT

Containment is a foreign concept for many traditional parents. The notion of holding a child instead of spanking or "putting the fear of God" into him is often regarded as molly-coddling, babying or indulging. Chapter 6 of Dynamics and the book, *Holding Time,* by Martha Welch provide valuable insights into the process of loving submission rather than forcing the child to yield to the power of a bigger person.

Loving containment of a child's unacceptable behaviors is the key to limiting those behaviors while at the same time conveying a message of love to the child. Resorting to punishment and extreme efforts at control will only result in deepened hostility and resentment between child and the parent, producing an angry, hostile, defiant or depressed child, and later, an unhappy control oriented person.

The thing that makes this taming process so effective is that the parent allows the child to vent rage and get the rage out of the his system. When the parent refrains from retaliating, the anger is not put back into the child, but when a parent uses anger to defeat a child's anger, the child will experience an infusion of more anger and the process of conscience development will be slowed or in some cases stopped. Children who are permitted to experience their rage without retaliation from their parent are far less bound up with anger and hatred than otherwise, and will thus in the long run be more apt to seek the parent's approval and love.

PRINCIPLE 10

Temperance is learned by example and experience, not taught by way of instruction, criticism or insistence.

CONSCIENCE: A SUMMARY

Conscience development is a process. It begins in early toddlerhood and proceeds throughout the first four or five years of a child's life. The repeated application of loving containment for a child's anger and hatred will lead to a well-tempered character. This process of character tempering is similar to the tempering steel in the physical world.

Steel is tempered by applying enough heat to soften, but not melt it. This heated steel is stressed and reshaped in some way, only to be quenched in water or some other liquid before repeating the process over again. The ongoing repetition of heating and quenching results in a form of steel that "gives" rather than breaks, that is resilient rather than brittle, that resists corrosion rather than rusts. This creates a varitey of steel that is far superior to non-tempered steel or the simple combination of its elementary parts (iron and carbon).

Such it is with people and the process of strengthening character. Each time a child becomes enraged, the child experiences the searing fire of inner turmoil and enormous self-doubt; when the parent (mother at first, father later), contains this child with the ongoing reassurance that the fires of anger, rage and hatred are not life threatening, the parent is reaching the inner spirit of that child. When the child's rage has dissipated, he or she is essentially removed from the direct heat of the inner fires; the addition of the parent's loving countenance throughout these experiences quenches the searing heat of hate and self-doubt within the child and leaves the child feeling loved and filled with the knowledge that these very difficult feelings can be tolerated and overcome.

The ongoing repetition of this process of tempering is how a strong character is built within a child. And once a strong character has been formed, it will be present throughout the life cycle.

Worksheet

CONSCIENCE FORMATION

1. What is/was your reaction to your child's anger and hatred?

2. When you look back, what was your mother's reaction to your anger and hatred? What was your father's reaction?

3. Does it make sense to you that compassion should be held out to an angry child, or do you believe in strict punishment for controlling a child's behaviors?

4. Think about how your mother and father dealt with their anger toward one another. How does their way of dealing with strong emotions compare with your way of handling them?

5. Have you ever had an argument with your best friend? What happened that lead up to the argument? What happened afterward? Did you make up? Did the relationship deepen or dissolve? How does this compare with what happens between you and your child when he is angry with you?

6. Do you believe your child has a solid conscience? What makes you think this?

7. What one thing might you change to improve your ability to facilitate an emotional reconciliation with your child?

4

POWER AS STRONG MEDICINE

PRINCIPLE 11

Power compensates for and alleviates the shame that accompanies failure. Never underestimate an angry child's desire to thwart a parent's authority. If the only power he can experience is the power to upset or anger the parent, then that is what he will do; neither punishments, consequences, nor self-suffering will deter the angry child.

POWER: A WORKING DEFINITION

Most people have an intrinsic understanding of power, but a formal definition can be useful. The American Heritage Dictionary defines power as follows:

- the ability or capacity to perform or act effectively
- a specific capacity, faculty, or aptitude
- strength or force exerted or capable of being exerted; might
- the might of a nation, political organization, or similar group
- the ability or official capacity to exercise control; authority
- a person, group, or nation having great influence or control over others
- forcefulness; effectiveness

These are just a few ways in which we define power within our language.

Interpersonal power can be simply defined as exercising one's influence over another person in an effort to change things from what they are to what one would like them to be. These changes include another's thoughts, words, deeds, feelings, attitudes, movements, or many other things, even character traits. Often in interpersonal relationships, the exercise of power over another has harmful effects. Wives and husbands, families and siblings, children and parents, bosses and employees struggle for power throughout much of their relationships. It is easy for people "in power" to forget that as good as it might feel to "get one's way," there can be an accompanying feeling of defeat and failure for those who don't.

POWER: STRONG MEDICINE AGAINST SHAME

As already noted, when parents are effective at setting and maintaining limits, children experience the feeling of shame (failure) marked by frustration, anger, or rage. For the most part, this is as it should be. A child does not want to accept parental limits, nor does she like to feel like a "loser" after a struggle with a parent. Many people (especially children) feel "beaten down" when they don't get their way with another, and one of the quickest and most effective ways to remedy this feeling (i.e., the feeling of failure or shame) is to somehow achieve power over the person seen as the more powerful. With peers, children might strike out at one another; with parents, a child might escalate the intensity of her protests against the parent's efforts, thus creating anger and frustration within the parent.

When a child rebels against a parent, both find themselves in a power struggle. A parent must be able to resolve these power struggles in favor of the child, yet maintain parental authority. If the parent cannot do so, one of two things will happen. The child will either win, or the child will lose. If the child wins, he will feel victorious, but with significant anxiety due to the fact that parents are not supposed to be defeated (see Principle 18); if the child loses, he will internalize this failure as shame, which if repeated over and over again will become "toxic shame" (i.e., deeply ingrained feelings of inferiority and self-doubt) and his core sense of self-worth will be damaged (see *Shame: a Brief Dissertation*, page 133).

PARENT POWER: "BECAUSE I SAID SO."

PRINCIPLE 12

> *Parents should limit expectations to what can actually be achieved; expecting a child to conform to parental ideals of what she should be and do is a sure way to experience*

> *heartache and frustration. Parents should eliminate the phrase "do it because I said so" from their vocabulary. It's a waste of time and energy.*

Throughout this book it has been emphasized that a parent needs to be in control of all situations in the home. This need to be in control, however, cannot be construed as license for the parent to assume control with brutish or abusive means. The principles put forth in *Dynamics* are designed to help parents learn to let go of interpersonal control (coercion) and resort to controlling the environment, thus creating and sustaining a sense of control and mastery for the child in his world. More simply, the child is compelled to make decisions and seek acceptable ways to meet goals.

One of the bigger mistakes made by parents is the use of the phrase "because I said so." This phrase is often a parent's response anytime that a child questions a request, demand, or limit imposed by the parent. When a child repeatedly hears "because I said so," she will emotionally and behaviorally "push" the parent to distraction, and the parent will continue to repeat "because I said so." Eventually the child will either acquiesce (often because the parent escalates the threat of angry retribution) or will find a way to get the parent to change her mind about the issue at hand.

When a child acquiesces, it is often grudgingly and with resentment. The task might get completed, but often it will be done poorly; and many times the child will harbor negative feelings that can reemerge in the form of resistance, noncompliance, and/or a spirit of non-cooperation at some point in the future. This sets up the parent to feel more anger and frustration in upcoming attempts at parenting.

When the child is able to initiate an argument with the parent, she is either making headway toward dissuading the parent from the parent's original goal, or is attempting to push the parent to get angry and punitive, which can later lead to feelings of guilt on the part of the parent (see the following section). Either way, the child can convince herself that she has won a victory over the parent.

The parental attitude of "because I said so" is further damaging in that the parent becomes a dictator in the child-parent relationship and within the family system. This can lead to feelings of resentment in the child and can lead to a child who seeks revenge in underhanded ways. Often a child will resort to passively angering the dictatorial parent and seek an ally in the non-dictatorial part of the system. When this occurs, one parent is set up to be the tyrant in the family and the other is set up to be the rescuing counter-balance by protecting the child from the tyrannical parent (usually out of guilt, pity or anger). This undermines the rightful authority (albeit abusive) of the controlling parent, and leaves the family system in an extremely compromised position with psychological bids for power taking place in a triangular manner, often with various family members pitted one against the other. (It is important to note that either parent can be the controlling [or rescuing] parent in a dysfunctional family situation; the roles are not gender specific.)

The solution to this problem, however, is ***not*** simple adherence to the wishes of the dictator. The optimum solution would be for the dictator to learn that he is indeed a dictator and that his need for control is damaging; it is further important for him to learn more amenable techniques for maintaining authority (see *Win/Win Parenting*, page 156).

As the dictatorial parent is learning to be less of a tyrant, the counterbalancing parent (the rescuer and protector) has to learn to be more demanding and less pity-oriented in the parent-child relationship. Both parents have to learn to be more supportive of one another. In the end, the dictator needs to be more like the rescuer, and the rescuer needs to be more like the dictator; when this middle ground is reached, harmony results.

When a parent is vying to have control for control's sake and resorts to "because I sad so" she is revealing a lack of awareness of anything else to do except use anger and/or coercion to be in control. Naturally, this leads the child to do the same. When the parent has only this one tool for dealing with difficult situations, a child quickly finds ways to outwit, outdo, and/or outpower the parent with resistance and/or defiance. These types of situations lead to a child who learns to gain power for the sake of gaining power; any power will do, at any cost, even self-destruction (see Principle 11).

KID POWER: POWER FOR POWER'S SAKE

Many family situations involve parents who are overly strict or harsh in their parenting applications. As noted above, the ongoing repetition of this type of parenting will yield a child who will harbor resentments and grudges against the controlling parent. Children are subject to all the strengths and weaknesses afforded to persons by human nature; to discount this by way of the notion that "she's only a kid" is a sure way to get "blind-sided" by that child's bids for power (usually in the form of anger).

Many people are tempted to say, "so what if the child is angry, why should I be concerned about *his* anger?" Parents often don't realize that children have just as much power as do they; it's just that children are not given the same authority as the parent. When children get angry and stay angry, they develop a variety of ways to retaliate against the adult whom is seen as creating that anger. When this occurs, parents keep trying harder and harder to gain the upper hand in the relationship only to discover that the child has again "won" simply by not giving in to the parent's wishes. In the end parents find themselves drained of any good emotional energy and despite their efforts, still at the mercy of the angry child.

Many controlling parents attempt to set and maintain limits without giving much thought to the process, and then after setting limits, the parent often leaves himself open to a change of heart due to guilt. Sometimes this guilt occurs as soon as the child begins her protest and the parent begins to feel that he is being unkind or unloving. The parent then gives in very quickly because he does not want to be seen as mean. Other times, parental guilt doesn't occur until after the parent has battled with the child and has lost his temper. Usually, during these occasions the parent first sees the child as ungrateful and/or self-centered, then the parent becomes punitive and harsh, and ultimately lashes out at the child. In most cases, this angry state of mind dissipates quickly for the parent, then guilt sets in. This parental guilt becomes the source of an inordinate amount of power to the child.

When a parent gives in to guilt, he giving in to the child's anger, and thus succumbs to the child's bid for power over the parent. This is how parents unwittingly condition their children to become manipulative, excessively demanding, entitled, and spoiled. Consider the following vignette:

> Remember Daphne from the supermarket in chapter three? She is now seven and is becoming a big girl.
>
> Daphne is left at home one Saturday morning with dad because mom is attending an art class. Today, Daphne has had a particularly bad morning. She refused to eat her cereal for breakfast and would only eat a toaster pastry instead; she didn't like the clothes mother had picked for her, so dad let her wear others; she refused to brush her teeth, wash her face, and she would not let dad comb her hair. Yet, after all this fuss, she settles into playing with her baby dolls.
>
> At about mid-morning Daphne asks her dad if she could have a new Barbie doll because Susie Who-Gets-All-She-Wants got a new doll yesterday. Dad says *No.* He tells Daphne that she has been misbehaving, and that little girls who misbehave don't get rewarded. Daphne starts to cry; dad tells her to stop; she doesn't; she cries harder and becomes angry at her dad; she calls him a big meanie, and promptly informs him that she hates him.
>
> Dad tells her to go to her room, but she refuses and raises the pitch of her anger to near volcanic proportions. Dad loses

> his patience and orders Daphne to go to her room; he is now calling her names (spoiled brat, little snot) and has begun threatening to spank her if she doesn't get into her bedroom.
>
> She taunts him; he becomes irate. He reaches out, grabs her, and whacks her several times on the backside. At this point, she runs to her room screaming that she is going to call Children's Services and report her dad for child abuse. She slams the door and locks dad out of her room. He tells her to open the door; she screams *No*. He then pushes the door open, breaking the door jamb, and finds his daughter hiding under her bed, sobbing.
>
> He is suddenly struck by the outright absurdity of the situation and retreats to the living room. He can hear Daphne's sobs; he begins to cool down; he starts to feel like a complete idiot. He watches about 20 minutes of TV and sees an ad for Barbie dolls at the local department store.
>
> He goes back to Daphne's room and starts fixing the door; while doing so, he tells her that there is a Barbie doll sale at the store and asks her if she would like to run over there and get one after he fixes the door. She perks up; says *–es* with just a hint of shyness, and gives her daddy a kiss on the cheek. An hour later, she is back in her room playing with her dolls which now number one more than they did earlier in the morning.

The above scenario (or some variation of it) happens far too often in families throughout the country. Often times, the details may differ in intensity and duration, but nonetheless, these dynamics occur. An examination of these events can lead to some interesting interpretations of what is going on between Daphne and her father.

First, Daphne appears to subtly defeat her father's authority; she won't do the simple things that dad wants her to do. Then she settles in to her routine, an indication that there is really nothing the matter with her ability to behave well if she chooses to do so. Next, she starts her bid for her new doll. Throughout the exchange it appears that Daphne is on the short end, but in the final analysis, she obtains the object of her initial desire, the Barbie doll, and with it, success by way of the power of her anger, her determination, lack of guilt and her previous experiences of her father.

The above seems very cunning for a relatively small child, but the fact is a child will often lose the ability to respond in a conscionable manner when feeling angry and resentful over losing a battle with the parent. This leads to the very natural response of trying to find some way to defeat the parent. In the above illustration, it is actually the father who is teaching his daughter to be cunning and devious due to his need for control. His failure to be effective as a parent results from his need to get his way, which is exactly the same thing his daughter is trying to accomplish. As seen above, this leads to a child who learns to manipulate people to give her things by making them hate her and then preying on their guilt for doing so.

Situations in families can get very bad due to excessive use of anger and control on the part of a parent. In the story above, Daphne's manipulation of father resulted in his eventual defeat. If father had held onto his anger and not given in as he did, Daphne might have gotten her mother involved or resorted to some destructive act to sway her father. **Note:** When behaviors escalate to include violent tendencies (directed either at others or self) it is time to seek professional assistance.

OTHER "POWER TOOLS" (ABUSES OF POWER)

There are a variety of methods used by parents and children to gain power over one another. Methods of power are passed down from parent to child, from generation to generation. A major problem with this process is that most parents learn only one method of gaining power from their parents, and it is this one method that is employed as their primary tool for motivating their own children to comply with their parental authority. Some of these tools are outlined below.

Guilt

As seen above, guilt is often the principle way that a child manipulates a parent to give into her will. But guilt is also an extremely popular method employed to get children to come under the direction of the parents. Guilt works for a parent when a child is well-attached and does not want to disappoint the parent by daring to be independent or oppositional; these children have a strong need to be good. They are often compliant to a fault, but very often have difficulty, later, as parents trying to cope with the rigors of parenting a strong-willed child; it is then that the parent learns that the use of guilt fails to provide the motivation they seek.

Many children disciplined by way of guilt experience numerous and various ailments throughout their lives that result from neurotic tendencies created by buried feelings of anger and hostility (e.g., addictions, compulsions, obesity, chronic illnesses, and sexual promiscuity).

Some standard phrases used by guilt inducing parents are:

- If you loved me you'd do this for me
- Please do this for me, just this one time
- Your sister doesn't fuss like this when asked to do things
- You want people to like you, don't you?
- You should be ashamed of yourself and shame on you
- Your father would really like it if you went to church this morning
- What would the neighbors think if they saw how you are acting?
- Don't ever bring shame on this family by getting into trouble
- I always thought you would get better grades than this
- I can't handle it when you act like this

Fear

Another popular tool for gaining a child's compliance is the use of fear. This is often done by the direct application of anger or the threat of anger to situations in which a parent might have trouble gaining control or compliance. Although fear is not recommended as a primary tool for effective parenting, it is an important part of development for most people. Ordinarily, the mere size of the parents in relationship to a child is imposing to the point that a child is naturally predisposed to be afraid; when anger is added to the mix, fear can quickly become terror.

FEAR AND MOTHERS

PRINCIPLE 13

A mother's power in a child's world is the power of love; a mother's use of anger rarely creates fear in a child, but instead leaves a child feeling anxious and concerned that "mother doesn't love me anymore." Mothers must find a way to discipline while maintaining an attitude of approval and love.

A child does not typically fear that mother can or will harm her physically, and if there is a fear of physical danger, it is foreshadowed by a far greater power possessed by the mother: the power to withhold love. When a mother uses anger to instill fear in her child, she is imitating what she has learned about gaining power from men (traditionally, the father is seen as the parent who uses anger as his vehicle for control). Typically, mother is not feared as a physical threat; rather she is feared on the level of withholding love and approval. When a mother becomes angry, the bond between mother and child is weakened and the child becomes anxious. When a child gets anxious, she typically moves toward the mother; however, when this anxiety is a result of a mother's bid for power, the opposite can occur. The child will be more likely to become defiant or withdrawn in an effort to avoid being manipulated by the mother.

Mother needs to learn that her approval is one of the most desired things in the world for her developing child. Mother must learn, as does the father, to use this tool by not using it. Mother must know that her approval is so important to her child that the child will strive to get and keep mother's approval with great effort, as long as mother is not trying to use this approval as a tool to gain power. When a mother attempts to use anger and the removal of approval as her primary strategies for gaining compliance, the child will quickly gather defenses against this process.

Anger and fear when employed by mother in an effort to gain compliance will generally result in a child who loses respect for the mother. When a child feels lack of love or disapproval from the mother, the child loses his desire to care about others. Many times, it is this sort of dynamic that will lead to behavioral and attitudinal problems both inside and outside the home.

Mother must learn the principles of dynamic parenting and employ them with consistent gentleness, respect and acceptance. The child who learns that he must conform to a kind mother's wishes, learns to gain his mother's approval by way of compliance. On the other hand, the child who learns that he must conform to the guilt-inducing mother will become bitter and resistant to the notions of love and compassion throughout life.

FEAR AND FATHERS: THE POWER OF FEAR AND THE FEAR OF POWER

PRINCIPLE 14

Fathers should refrain from the use of anger or fear as a way of controlling a child or teaching him a lesson; anger-oriented parenting results in a child who is unable to think clearly, thus compromising his ability to "learn his lesson."

It appears that fathers have a two-fold source of power when considering fear. First, as with mothers, father's have the power of love.

Many, many children respond to their fathers in the same manner as their mothers with regard to the fear of losing the father's love. And, as with mothers, this fear needs to be recognized yet not used as a tool for gaining control and compliance from the youngster.

Often, the evidence of the power of a father's love can be seen in situations of divorce in which the father is the absentee parent. Children often fall all over themselves to be ready when dad is coming to pick them up for the weekend, yet won't get out of bed in the morning to go shopping for new clothes with mother (the custodial parent). This sort of dynamic can fuel resentment on the part of mother who, after all, provides the vast majority of daily support for the child. The phenomenon of "Disneyland Dad" is a very real concern for many mothers and much of the hard work of discipline, rules, and limits that is done throughout the week by the mother is undone on weekends with dad. Some non-custodial parents will deliberately spoil a child during visitations as a way to exact revenge upon the custodial parent. Children can be severely damaged by such activity.

Second, a child fears the father on a physical level. It is natural for a child to fear her father's size and demeanor, and for generations many men have used anger or the threat of anger to gain control of family relationships. In these situations, the child's fear of losing father's love is compounded by the fear that dad might impose serious damage to the child's physical well-being.

In the mid-twentieth century, the American family was organized around two basic rules: Dad makes the rules, and don't make dad angry. In some ways these rules still apply, but in today's world the last thing that a father should do is to use anger as a method for control of the family. Paternal anger puts the fear of God into children, and fathers should be careful with the application of anger to engender this fear. As noted above, a man has the ability to put fear into a child by way of his presence alone; the existence of this hint of fear can be molded into a desire to do the right thing as long as the father is aware of its presence within the child and chooses to refrain from employing it.

The use of paternal anger in parenting leads to one of two outcomes that are at opposite ends of a continuum. On the one hand, paternal anger can result in a child whose spirit is trapped, the child who will obey blindly and cower when chided or chastised, while his or her sense of self-determination is clearly compromised. On the other hand, a father's use of anger can lead to a rebellious, noncompliant, and/or defiant child who will desperately try to prove to the parent that she cannot be frightened (coerced) into compliance, often exclaiming self-determination in a very visible yet destructive manner.

As a child grows and develops, he may shift from pole to pole within the continuum; for example, a young girl who was a good little girl throughout her early years due to fear of father can often turn to anger, drugs, sex, and other forms of negative acting-out when dad is no longer a threat. A boy who was a rebellious teenager and was full of hatred can grow up, get married and become a tyrant in his own family.

The best use of paternal fear in raising children is to be aware of its existence but to refrain from calling on it for control. When fear (paternal anger) is used, the father loses credibility as a viable authority figure because he shows that he lacks restraint, creativity, finesse, or respect. A father who lacks emotional control of himself soon becomes a toothless lion or a raging tyrant.

ANGER AND POWER

Anger and power have gone hand-in-hand since the beginning of civilization. In many ways nearly all people and civilizations have agreed on this: when all else fails get mad, and when you get mad, make sure you can defeat the object of your anger.

Anger should be viewed as a necessary fact of life within every person, but angry behavior should be viewed as a mistake. The responsible person should learn to apologize and work to reduce both the frequency and intensity of her anger in future interactions. A parent should not insist on an apology from a child, but should always apologize when he or she (the parent) uses anger in the parent-child relationship. If an attitude of firmness, yet acceptance, is expressed toward the angry child, the child will eventually learn to feel guilt after getting angry and will in turn learn to apologize as part of the process of relating with other people.

It cannot be emphasized strongly enough, nor often enough, that the use of anger in the parent-child relationship is extremely harmful to the welfare of the child. Angering at children should be considered the first cardinal sin of parenting. Healthy children will grow from families in which anger has been mastered by the parents to the point that the other family members will feel safe. This safe feeling results in children who are able to express and vent their own anger throughout the maturation process without the fear of parental retribution; children who will, in the end, grow out of their need for anger and proceed to their positions of authority in their own families.

Overcoming anger in interpersonal relationships is a matter that must be addressed by each person who has this problem. People tend to be angry in relationships for two different yet related reasons: a person is an angry person and knows only anger as the way to do things, and the person is basically a non-angry person who doesn't know what else to do and falls back on anger. Much of the reason for the preparation of Dynamics has been to reach people who get angry at their children because they don't know what else to do; for the angry parent, it is recommended that he or she take a serious inward look and decide if there is enough reason to make changes within the self. If so, it is likely that professional assistance will be needed to foster that change.

CORPORAL PUNISHMENTS: SPANKING, HITTING, SLAPPING

Corporal punishments should be avoided by all means possible. There is no room in effective parenting for hitting or slapping.

Some parent educators allow for the use of spanking as long as it is done in a reasonable, moderated, and consistent manner for only a select few undesirable behaviors. It is held that corporal punishment is effective at changing behaviors because it instills fear in the child. It is this fear that provides the internal mechanism for the child's behavioral control. The use of fear for control has never been effective for teaching love and restraint, harmony and cooperation.

Another reason for writing *Dynamics* is to help a parent learn that anger need not be the cornerstone for control within the family. *The Dynamics of Powerful Parenting* is about working with children in a containing way to create a spirit of cooperation rather than a aura of fear, blind obedience, or blind disobedience.

Any parent who believes that physical punishments are necessary for maintaining order in a family's life is operating out of an archaic and primitive approach to parenting. In most cases, the use of corporal punishment is a sign of an overabundance of anger within the family system. Parents who find themselves in this state should consider seeking a counselor or therapist to help them deal with their anger.

POWER AND THE WESTERN WAY: A BRIEF SUMMARY

As has been noted several times throughout *Dynamics,* power and its moderation are essential to healthy family living and to the development of healthy people.

There is a story that has been told about mustanging in the Old West that displays the differences between the white man (the cowboy) and natives of The North American Tribes (the American Indian). This story reveals the basic difference between coercive versus considerate parenting.

Most modern Americans have seen at least one movie in which some cowboy mounts a wild mustang and rides the horse until it is broken; the cowboy can then ride the mustang at will. The breaking method is fast, furious, sometimes dangerous, but in the end, effective.

What most people have never seen is the way that some American Indian tribes went about the business of "breaking" their ponies.

Once a horse (pony) was captured, it was contained in a holding environment (a corral). The brave who was to be the rider of this horse would begin the taming process by first getting the horse's attention with a whistle and wave from a distance. The brave would not approach the horse at first, but would simply let the horse see him. After a few days, the brave would begin to approach the horse, still maintaining some distance, but approaching nonetheless. After a few more days the brave would finally reach the corral and began to hold out food for the horse; as the trust between man and horse grew, the horse moved closer to accept the food.

After the horse had accepted the food, the brave would venture into the corral and would reenact the approach pattern again, this time culminating with the brave feeding the horse while touching it. Next, the brave would stroke the horse's nose, and a few days later would stroke its flanks. Soon the brave would be able to put his hands on the horse's back and begin to put pressure upon it. This would give way to the brave being able to drape himself over the horse, and shortly thereafter, mount it. There would be no kicking, no bucking, and no coercion. The rider and the horse became one with another.

In the end, both the white man and the Indian accomplished the same task, but the process employed by each was clearly different. When raising children, especially today's children, the most effective way to achieve healthy human beings is for parents to learn to tame and train their children rather than break and control them. The lessons of patience and process must be employed by today's parents in a spirit of trust and cooperation.

Worksheet

POWER

1. Do you consider yourself a powerful person? Why or why not?

2. What is your primary method for executing your authority with the child or children in your family?

3. How did your father discipline boys? girls?

4. How did your mother discipline boys? girls?

5. Did you feel safe enough with your parents to express your own negative feelings?

6. Do you think that ongoing discussions about the dynamics of power would have been a help to you as a young person growing up?

7. Reflecting on power, what is the one thing that you must absolutely change about yourself to become a better parent?

5

WINNING IS A GOOD THING

PRINCIPLE 15

Parents need to be aware that their children must experience the ability to "win" in the child-parent relationship; this victory must be fostered by the parent within reasonable tolerances for limits and boundaries. This creates a feeling of success within the child and results in less need for achieving power for power's sake (Principle #11).

THE BEAUTY OF WIN/WIN PARENTING

Parents deal with discipline issues from toddlerhood through adolescence. The techniques and strategies used by parents in large measure mold the character of their children.

Traditional parenting techniques (the 1950s model and prior) do not work in today's world because they are based on the fear of immediate punishment. Today's children have been able to bypass this fear by way of the civil rights movement in the late 1960s and early 1970s. Many civil rights battles were waged in those days, and not the least of which concerned the rights and protection for children. Today's children have grown up knowing the meaning of democracy and have learned how to use it for their own ends.

Modern American children have for the most part been raised in an extremely indulgent society, and have grown to expect indulgence as part of their lives. The fact is, except for the most impoverished, children today have far more at their disposal than any previous generation in the history of humanity. Yet it seems our children do not appreciate what they have; they seem always to want more, and they seem to want to do less to get it.

Win/Win Parenting (see p. 156), is a very simple and logical way to get children to do things. The child's dependencies (the raw materials for Win/Win Parenting) are present from the time a child is born; the problem is that parents have used them incorrectly.

One of the worst enemies of a parent is unrealistic expectations. Consider the things parents expect of their children: to clean their rooms without being asked, to eat all their peas and like it, to do the dishes without being reminded, to spontaneously wash their faces and hands when dirty, to vacuum floors because they need vacuumed, to complete their homework without argument, to go to bed without resistance, keep their clothes clean, like the foods that are good for them, and so on. The fact is, that if children did these things, they would not be children, they would be adults, and more than that, they would be ideal adults.

When parents pause to take time to think about what they want from their children, they often find that they seek only the completion of a particular task or chore; few think about the process they expect to occur, and even fewer think about the process that is occurring when trying to get things done. Yet in the end, what most parents want from their children is reasonable; it's the way they go about getting it that is not.

There is nothing wrong with thinking that a child should clean his or her room, but there is something very unrealistic with thinking that this should be done automatically without being told, or that it he will do it immediately when given instruction. No one likes to be coerced or criticized, to be put down, and/or yelled at (made to feel shame) because something hasn't been done just the way, or just when, someone else wants it to be done. Children are people, and they ought to be respected as such. Children should at least be accorded the same respect as is given to complete strangers in the workplace or at the shopping mall; however, along with this respect comes the child's responsibility to learn to yield to the authority of the parent. Win/Win Parenting does just that.

Win/Win Parenting is a contractual form of parenting in which the parent sets the terms of the contract in advance because the parent holds all the cards. Most parents fail to get a child to do things for the simple reason that the child is not motivated to cooperate with the parent at the time the parent wants the cooperation.

One of the more disconcerting aspects of children today is that they seem to want everything and they seem to want it now; even more dismaying is that they usually get it. Most parents dislike seeing their children want for newer and more things, but they seem to like it even less when they cry, complain, or throw accusations at parents for not giving into demands. As a result of this ongoing clamoring and demanding, many parents want to say *No* as their first response to a child's requests. Parents usually do this as a response to their own distaste for the child's apparent sense of entitlement. Too many times, however, a parent will succumb to the child's escalated efforts to attain whatever it is that he wants from the parent. This type of behavior on the part of the parent only serves to fuel the fires of the child's power, and increases parental resentment and disappointment.

PRINCIPLE 16

> Yes *is a far more powerful motivator than any threat, coercion or punishment can ever be. Use it wisely with conditions and with sincerity. Avoid punishments for noncompliance at all costs.*

Parents must learn to say —*es* as their first response to a child's request, and then add "When…you do this for me." If a parent will learn this one simple shift in her approach to her child's requests, she will experience the gratification of watching the child make decisions based on need rather than mere want or opposition to her. In terms of power, when a parent wants a child to do something, the child has the control over the outcome of the situation because the child can refuse, and thus, the parent is rendered powerless; the child holds the power in the interaction. If, however, the child wants the parent to do something for him, then it is the parent who determines whether this wish is granted, and therefore the power is restored to its rightful place with the parent.

Many parents want to refute the notion that '—*es*, When...' is a feasible intervention by arguing that the child still has the option to refuse to perform the task, or that a child should not have to be asked to do something that clearly needs to be done. Both are indeed true, but only if immediate compliance is the goal for the parent; however, if the parent makes *the enforcement of the contract* his or her goal in the exchange, then there is no failure possible unless the parent gives in. (See Win/Win Parenting Intervention in appendix.)

No becomes the last word in the execution of the win/win contract; it is the "No, I will not do this for you" or "No, you may not have my permission to do that" which is used to meet the child's choice to refuse to do the task; these conditions cannot be broken as long as the parent stands by the contract.

Consider the following:

Daphne and her father are together again on another Saturday morning and mom is again at Art class. A few months have elapsed since their riotous Barbie doll incident and Daphne is now eight years old. In the time that has passed, dad has read his copy of Dynamics, studied up on the workings of Win/Win Parenting, and has been practicing in a variety of ways the principles of powerful parenting. He has reflected many times on his mistakes in the earlier episode and is ready for a new day with Daphne.

Dad awakens Daphne and she refuses to get out of bed; dad lets her sleep. When she does get up, she is ravenously hungry. Dad informs her that he had already fixed breakfast two hours ago. She insists that she wants to eat and becomes demanding. Dad says he'll be glad to fix her pancakes or cereal as soon as she gets her teeth brushed, face washed, hair combed, and dressed for the day. She thinks about it for a moment and says "Okay, dad, pancakes."

After her breakfast, dad asks her what she would like to do for the rest of the morning. She indicates that she wants to go shopping for a new pair of shoes just like dad had promised her the previous evening. Dad says, "That will be fine; we'll leave after you get your clothes picked up from the floors in the bathroom and your bedroom; also you'll have to clear the table and put the dirty dishes from your breakfast into the sink." (What he doesn't tell her is that he has a few errands to run while he is out.) She looks at dad and says, "Okay."

Daphne is ready to leave in less than twenty minutes. On the way to the shoe store dad tells Daphne that he has only thirty dollars to spend for shoes this morning and that she will have to fit the shoes she wants into his budget. She begins to moan "that's not fair;" he quietly and matter-of-factly tells her that her only other option is for her to get no shoes at all. He also tells her that he has to get his errands completed before going to the shoe store. She gets a little huffy, dad stays cool; she thinks for a minute and says (with some resignation), "Okay dad."

Dad and Daphne continue throughout the rest of the morning without a major incident. On those occasions when Daphne becomes irritated or upset, dad simply remains calm, tells her what he is and is not willing to do, and allows her to choose if she wants the outing to continue or if she wants to

> go home. On this day, Daphne continues to choose to finish the outing in part because dad (in his new-found wisdom) has saved the purchase of the shoes for the very last thing to do before returning home.

As can be seen from the above rendition of Daphne and dad's "new Saturday," there have been some changes. First of all, dad seems calmer and less insistent of getting things his way; second, dad seems to be able to anticipate Daphne's needs and wants. Third, Daphne is trapped; she wants certain things that only her dad can provide for her, and she can't get them unless she works with dad to get them. Fourth, Daphne thinks about her choices before she makes them; she seems to ponder the various outcomes and chooses the path that gets her what she wants; she doesn't have to resort to "power at any cost" to feel in control of her life with her father. Lastly, dad and Daphne have a good time; she is getting what she wants and he is getting what he wants; together they are happy with one another, yet dad is the boss, she is the kid; that's the way it should be.

Win/Win Parenting is useful in almost all parenting endeavors. Many times parents will have to become accustomed to using the technique in creative ways. For instance, consider another situation:

> Peter (a.k.a. Petulant Pete) Complainsalot, age 13, has been asked by his mother to mow the grass. After her request, mom goes on about her business, but is beginning to get a little put off by the fact that he has not moved toward completing this task. He doesn't want to go anywhere at the present, and mom is finding it very difficult to exercise a win/win strategy. So she grounds him to his room. Contrary to what she used to do, she is not grounding him for a specific time period. She simply informs him that he is grounded *until* he cuts the grass.
>
> Pete digs in his heels and determines that he will not cut the grass no matter what she says; she says nothing except, "You are grounded until you cut the grass." He won't violate the restriction because he knows mom will file an unruly complaint against him. He stays in his room all day Saturday; all day Sunday, and goes to his room immediately upon returning from school on Monday; he doesn't even come out for dinner. Mother still says nothing and she has made no effort to get someone else to cut the grass.
>
> Tuesday afternoon mother comes home from work to find the grass has been cut and the sidewalk edged. Pete is

> sitting in his room and mother goes to him and asks what's going on; he indicates that the guys are getting together to have a skateboarding competition at the church parking lot at 6 o'clock; "Can I go, now? I've cut the grass." Mom says, "Have a good time, and thank you for getting the yard finished; be back by nine."

Mother turned the above situation into a win/win contract when she restricted Pete to his room until he complied with her request to mow the lawn. This simple addition changed the situation from one in which the mother is trying to get the grass cut, to one in which she is effectively stopping him from leaving his room. The fact that he wants to be released from his room becomes the motivator for getting the chore done. Throughout such an exchange mother can remind herself that her son is making a choice about his immediate future; she has no reason to feel guilty because her son is choosing to suffer.

TRUST AND WIN/WIN PARENTING

Good parenting is about trust, and trust is about letting a child know where he stands with the parent at all times. It is the parent who teaches trust to the offspring, and it is the parent who must gain the trust of the youngster, not the other way around. Parents who punish their children because they "cannot be trusted" are in reality providing more cause to be untrustworthy (i.e., more anger). Time and again children are taught by parents that they have to behave in ways that will encourage trust within the parent for the child, yet parents continually break trust with the child in a variety of ways.

The parent who has trust problems with his child has a child who has trust problems with his parent. The parent who says, "Do as I say, not as I do," is clearly sacrificing trust for control in the parent-child relationship. The parent who drinks profusely, makes and breaks promises, then repeats this cycle is going to have a very difficult time with the child when he reaches adolescence. The parent who continually preaches to his son that he should not make the same mistakes as he made, yet persists in continuing to make those mistakes himself is teaching his child the essence of hypocrisy. The parent who espouses honesty, but steals paper and pens from her employer is setting an example that will likely result in mistrust in the child-parent relationship. The parent who punishes his child for smoking, yet consumes a pack and a half of cigarettes per day is looking for trouble with addictions in his child's life.

Trust is the cornerstone of all successful relationships. It doesn't come from just being a good enough parent to an infant. It comes from being a good enough parent to the child throughout the child's development. A parent must be trustworthy at all times. He must be on time; he must do what he says he's going to do, and he must be reliable. Trust grows between a parent and child; the first time trust is broken, it will take a little time and effort to win back that trust. When it is broken a second time, it will take more time and effort. When it is broken repeatedly, a pattern of mistrust emerges between the child and that parent that begins to characterize the relationship; it will require major efforts on an ongoing basis to repair such damage.

Win/Win Parenting strategies encourage trust in the parent-child relationship. This trust is built on a two-part foundation, each part interlocked with the other:

- The parent must be willing to negotiate with the child for the gratification of the child's wants and needs.
- The parent must follow through with the terms of the win/win contract.

The fact that a parent promises to gratify a child's wish when that child does something for the parent is just the first step to securing trust. It is when the parent follows through with the terms of the win/win contract that trust is solidified between the two parties.

It is important to remember that trust is not always a positive experience. Sometimes a child decides that she does not want to do what the parent requires, yet insists on getting the payoff. The parent must enforce the terms of the contract with an emphatic *No* and maintain that stance throughout the exchange. Although this is an unpleasant experience for the child, in the end the parent will win the child's trust (and respect).

A parent who gives in to a child after already saying *No* is breaking trust with that child. The parent may feel a temporary relief from guilt and pressure by yielding to the child's protestations and manipulations, but in the long run the child realizes serious psychological damage, not only due to the loss of trust, but because a child "knows" he is not supposed to be able to defeat his parents. (Principle 18: a child should not overpower his or her parent.)

SHAME

Another aspect of the use of Win/Win Parenting is the decrease in toxic shame (see *Shame and Self-esteem,* p. 135). Toxic shame builds up when critical and coercive parenting causes a child to internalize her natural shame.

The Win/Win Parenting system is based on the premise that a child has a choice of outcomes which are outlined in advance. This naturally yields more thought and deliberation on the part of the child. When a child knows in advance what price is affixed to the object of his desire, he will make a decision based on his internal measures (not the parent's).

For example: remember Petulant Pete?

> One Saturday morning Pete asked his mother if he could go and hang out with his chums at the grade school basketball court. His mother told him that he could go after he cleaned his room. Pete went back to watching TV and made no move toward cleaning his room, nor did he ask again to go visit with his friends.
>
> Later that day, Pete's friend, Billy, called him and asked him to go with him and his parents to a major league hockey game. Pete was thrilled at the offer. He immediately asked his mother if he could have her permission to do so; she said "Yes, but you'll have to get your room cleaned beforehand, and you'll have to empty all the trash into the trash bin and wheel it out to the curb for pickup the next morning."
>
> Pete completed the tasks to mother's specifications and departed on time for the hockey game with Billy. He was happy to go; his mother was happy to permit him to do so.

This example shows how the price (the parental condition) affixed to a certain request may be more than the child wants to pay at the time. In the first situation the payoff is not worth the cost, and therefore Pete chooses to forego the trip to the basketball court and remain home. Later, when afforded the opportunity to do something which he sees as more fun, he jumps at the chance. Mother capitalizes on this by reiterating her request to get the room cleaned and adds a little something extra. Pete gladly complies with mother's requests because the payoff is now worth the price

Adults make these kinds of decisions all the time. When buying food at the supermarket, clothes at the department store, cars at the dealership, sandwiches at the local fast food restaurant, and etc., people continually weigh the cost versus the benefit of their choices. Car salespeople do not say to someone who decides to pass on a certain car deal, "Hey, you have to buy this car, or I'm going to take your house away from you." Rather, they let the deal slip away and the person moves on to look for something else that better fits his needs and budget. There is no punishment for choosing one restaurant over another (aside from an occasional case of indigestion).

So it is with Win/Win Parenting strategies. The parent sets the contract for the exchange and the youngster has to decide the outcome with her behavior. If the young person chooses to let a particular contract pass, the parent allows for this with the knowledge that sometime in the future the child will return with another, more pressing request. The parent honors the decision of the youngster to pass in the short term, and by eliminating coercion, reduces the experience of shame in the interaction.

The fact that a parent is willing to let go of control in the moment gives the young person less reason to fight the parent, and therefore less reason to resist the parent in the future. The parental decision to honor a youngster's choice to refuse the parent is essentially a way to tell her that she is okay even though she appears noncompliant. Also, the child gets the message that it is okay to decide not to do something unless the conditions are right for her. The long-term benefits of using such a process of intervention yields children who are free thinkers with a strong sense of self-determination. Some parents criticize this tactic as a way to teach children that they don't have to comply with the parent; actually it is quite the opposite, it is a way to teach the child that authority will eventually prevail and that compliance is inevitable, but all the while teaching that life is about choices.

Parents need to realize there are very few have-to's in life. Many parents will maintain that dishes have to get done, that the grass has to be cut, that a room has to be cleaned, that the trash has to go out, and so forth. The world will not end because a few dishes need to be washed, or the grass gets cut on Friday instead of Tuesday, or that the trash barrel has to sit for another week. A parent must remember that a child is motivated on his own terms, not the parent's. When patience is exercised by the parent, many valuable lessons can be learned by the child.

WIN/WIN: TRUST AND PEER PRESSURE

It is important for parents to remember that teens are particularly vulnerable to peer pressure and that they will often act contrary to parental expectations when with peers due to the need to appear cool, or part of the crowd.

PRINCIPLE **17**

Peer pressure is a driving force in the life of a teenager; be aware that it is usually far more important to appease a peer than a parent. –et there will be times when your teen will want to be reeled in, but not able to convey it in words. It is the parent's job to help the youngster save face with peers by supplying an excuse to resist bad decisions.

A SPECIAL CASE FOR WIN/WIN

Sometimes children need a parent's help when facing peers, but will not directly ask for it due to the need to save face with other teens. Win/Win Parenting strategies are a perfect way to let a child behaviorally talk to a parent without having to use words that might endanger his sense of adolescent dignity.

Consider the following example:

> Jason Juxtaposition, a 16 year old sophomore, is ecstatic. He and some of his friends are planning a trip to a concert being performed by one of the most popular bands currently on tour. The concert will be in two weeks, but Jason wants to be sure that he gets things squared away with his parents because this will be his first outing with another youngster driving instead of a parent.
>
> Mr. and Mrs. J are pretty anxious about this trip, but they talk things over and decide that it is time to let Jason do more of the things that kids do at Jason's age. They sit down with Jason the day after his request and let him know (in fine win/win fashion) that he may attend the concert with his pals if he meets certain conditions.
>
> Mr. and Mrs. J have decided to set the price relatively high for this outing and let him know that he will have to do the dishes every evening without argument right up through the night of the concert; he will have to wash and vacuum dad's car; sweep the garage, and carry out the four boxes of trash that have been sitting in the basement since last winter.
>
> Jason gleefully agrees and complies with every request conveyed by his parents, except he does not remove the trash from the basement. On the evening of the concert he is dressed and ready to go, only to hear his father remind him that the boxes remain in the basement.
>
> Jason gets somewhat defensive with his dad and tells him that the guys are going to arrive soon and that he'll get to the trash tomorrow. Dad tells him that this was not the deal and that if the trash is not out of the house, he cannot leave. Jason gets very angry and becomes defiant with his father. He tells his dad that he's being petty and stupid, and that the trash can wait. Dad tells him one more time, if the trash is out, you can go; if not, you will stay home.
>
> Jason's friends drive up to the house. Jason is furious; he

> tells his friends that he can't go to the concert and gives one of them his ticket to sell for him on their way in. Jason tells the guys that his "asshole dad" will not let him go to the concert and that there's nothing he can do to change his dad's mind. They drive off on their merry way to attend the concert.
>
> The next day Jason's mom gets a call from one of her friends at the hairdresser's. She tells her that the very same boys with whom Jason was to attend the concert were pulled over for speeding on their way back from the concert. They were found to have drugs and alcohol in the car, and were detained by the police until their parents retrieved them. All of them will have to appear in Juvenile Court to face charges of possession of an illegal substance, under-aged consumption of alcohol, open containers of alcohol in a motor vehicle, and the driver will have to face a DUI.
>
> Jason's mother looks at him and says, "I guess in the end you were really lucky last night," and Jason replies with a simple, "Yeah, I guess so."

Whether Jason's parents know it or not, dad's strict adherence to the rules of Win/Win Parenting actually saved Jason from the same fate as his friends.

Over the two weeks before the concert, Jason's friends talked a lot about what they were planning, and it became obvious to Jason that he did not want to get involved in a drug and alcohol oriented adventure. Jason is a good kid and a deep thinker, but he wants to be accepted by his friends; if he chickens out on something planned by them, he fears being labeled a wimp or weenie. So he set up the little scene with his father the night of the concert, and counted on his dad to keep his word with him and to rigidly enforce the terms of the win/win contract. In other words Jason trusted his dad to be consistent and good to his word.

In the above situation Jason won by being able to shift the blame for his failure to attend the concert over to his father. His parents may have felt lucky, but Jason secretly felt very pleased that his instincts paid off and that he was right about avoiding the trouble that was brewing for that night.

FINAL THOUGHTS ABOUT WIN/WIN PARENTING

Win/Win Parenting works. It works especially well when a parent exercises patience and wisdom in his or her approach to noncompliance from a youngster (Win/Win Parenting, p. 156). It works when the parent makes win/win strategies part of his or her way of relating to the child without resorting to anger and coercion.

Parents who love their children and want to get along better with them will find Win/Win Parenting to be a great relief. Parents who desire to control and manipulate their child into compliance at any cost will find that Win/Win is no better a method than any other.

Win/Win Parenting is intended to represent a spirit of cooperation between a parent and a child. Parents must always remember that children are people and that people do not like to be pushed, shoved, forced, coerced, tricked or deceived into doing things for another. Win/Win Parenting is the parenting style that most closely approximates real world demands and conditions.

The use of win/win techniques throughout a child's development will result in a person who is willing to work for what she gets, and will be much more apt to pass a spirit of hard work, achievement, cooperation and respect onto the next generation.

Worksheet

WIN/WIN PARENTING

1. Have you read the win/win intervention (page 156)? If not, please do so before proceeding with this worksheet.

2. Are you, as the parent, willing to give up your notion that things should be done simply because you say so? Why or why not?

3. List five things that one of your children desires on a continual basis.

____

____

____

____

____

4. What is your typical response to these requests and demands?

5. List five things that you want from the same child on a regular basis:

____

____

____

____

____

6. What is that child's ordinary response to those requests?

7. How many times in a given week would you say that you and your child argue over chore completion? Describe the basic patterns that occur in those arguments.

8. Think about the last week with one of your children; describe the times you used anger to gain compliance with a request. Did you change your mind with regard to a limit or condition, after getting angry first? What are your thoughts about this?

9. Think of how Win/Win Parenting could have been used to prevent the anger and arguments, and describe how you might have done things differently.

10. Rate yourself with regard to parental consistency. Check your rating with your spouse or a close friend.

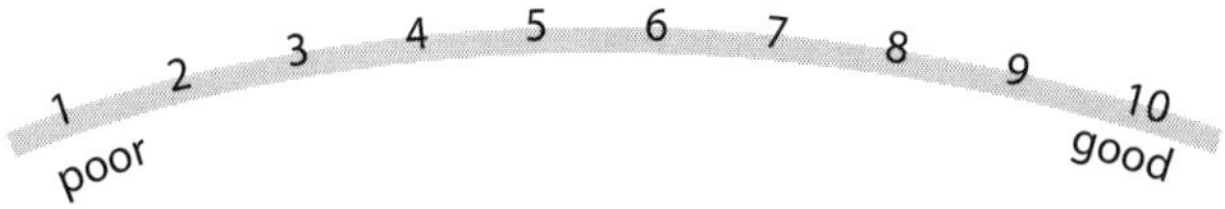

11. Do you feel a lot of guilt as a parent? Why? Why not?

12. Reconsider Jason's special case of win/win as outlined on pages 58-59. How do you think you would have handled that situation?

13. How trustworthy a parent are you?

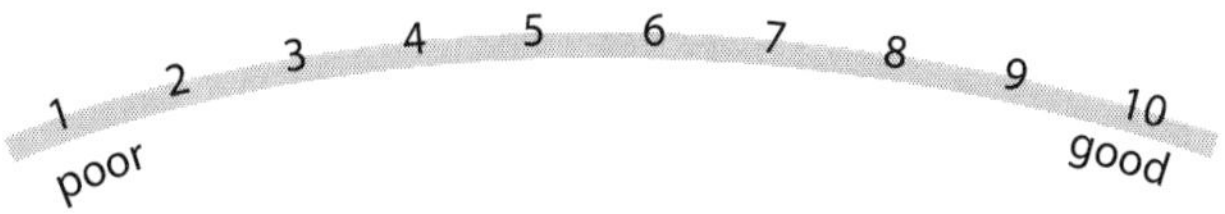

6

CONTAINMENT REVISITED

When the irresistible force meets the immovable object, the immovable object must be truly immovable.

PRINCIPLE 18

> *When a child overpowers a parent, both lose. The child who defeats his parent finds himself in a terrible paradox. On a conscious level he acquires control and thus an illusion of power; on an unconscious level he becomes terrified that his parents are so weak that even he can defeat them.*

A BACKUP PLAN

Win/Win Parenting is one of the most valuable tools a parent can employ for teaching a child how to develop a cooperative spirit with authority figures. It works because the procedure is designed to provide immediate rewards or consequences for whatever decision is reached by the child. The technique is based on trust, a clear awareness of the outcomes, and the knowledge that the parent cannot be overpowered. Win/Win functions in such a way as to mirror the nature of the real world.

Win/Win Parenting will not, however, always yield easy success in every situation. There will be times when a youngster will challenge the terms of the contract and attempt to go outside the limits as set forth by the parent. When these situations occur, the parent must have tools for containing the straying child.

Containment in wayward situations is achieved by the word *No;* the tools for containment are blocking and holding.

Blocking represents the notion that a parent can place himself in a position between the child and the child's goal at any particular moment. If a child refuses to adhere to the terms of a win/win contract, or if the child refuses to comply with a restrictive limit (e.g., "Stay in the bedroom"), then the parent must employ a "blocking" intervention. For instance, if the child wants the parent to leave him alone, the parent remains. If the child wants to get out of his room, the parent prevents this from occurring. If the child insists on watching TV, listening to music, using the telephone, or playing with toys, the parent will prevent these things from occurring until the parent is satisfied that the child has met whatever terms have been imposed (e.g., time-out, staying in a bedroom for fifteen minutes, or doing some chore or undesirable job).

It is important to remember that when containments are imposed upon a child, the child's personal boundaries are violated (see the discussion of limits and boundaries, page 11). Much care should be exercised by the parent to respect the personage of the child, and to show empathy toward the child in a containment situation. When a child is forced to accept a limit, he is losing freedom; this is rarely a pleasant experience for any person, let alone a wayward child.

CONTAINMENTS FOR YOUNGER CHILDREN (AGES 3 TO 9)

As noted in Chapter 3, the first and simplest containments of a child by the parent are the nonverbal containments of infancy. Mother's arms, the baby's swaddling clothes, and the baby's crib are the initial means for containing a child. Later, during toddlerhood, the word *No* becomes the vehicle for containment. The word *No* is the interactive verbal cue that alerts the child to the parent's desire to set and maintain a behavioral limit. When the parent utters *No,* there is no turning back; the parent must enforce the limit without fail.

PRINCIPLE 19

Inconsistency teaches your child that you cannot be trusted.

TIME-OUT

Another type of containment can be initiated at about three years of age: parents can initiate the use of *time-out* as a primary response to undesirable behaviors (see *Time-out,* page 139). Time-out starts out as a sort of game that goes on between child and parent and eventually becomes the mainstay of parenting in the first six years of the child's life. Time-out is used only in those cases where a child has committed some act that is unacceptable to the parent, such as name calling, hitting, swearing, acts of deliberate destruction, gross disrespect, lying, and stealing. Time-outs must be applied only to committed acts rather than refusals to comply with parental requests. Parents should be careful to note that time-out is not a viable response to defiance or oppositionalism; in other words, a young child should not be timed-out for refusing to obey a command or comply with a request.

Time-out becomes containment in the sense that it is a limiting factor in the child's ability to experience freedom. It is very important to remember that our society is based on the notion that freedom is more important that anything else, except when one person's freedom infringes upon another's. Therefore, when the child misbehaves in a manner that affects the well-being or comfort of others, the child must be limited.

The successful use of time-out is highly dependent upon the reason that the parent is employing its use. If the parent is using time-out as a way to respond to a behavior for the sake of providing a consequence, then successful completion of the time-out experience will in itself be considered a success. If, however, the parent is using time-out as a way to stop a child from doing a particular behavior in the future, it is very unlikely that use of time-out will be considered successful. Nothing that a parent does to a child will guarantee that the child will not reenact a given behavior in the future (Principle 3); therefore, if the goal is to change future behavior, time-out will be viewed as ineffective. For time-out to work, it must be viewed as a self-contained intervention in the moment, designed to restore order in the child-parent relationship.

GO TO YOUR ROOM!

There will be times when a child refuses to perform and complete a successful time-out. On these occasions (after about 42 months) the child can be sent to stay in her room (see *Go to —our Room!*, page 141) as the next level of containment for restricting the child's freedom. As long as the child is willing to remain in her room and accept the terms of the restriction (i.e., stay there until she agrees to comply with time-out or another activity, or until the completion of a specific amount of time) the child may choose to reject compliance with the initial parent request. In other words, if a child refuses to sit in time-out, she may continue to do so as long as she remains in the bedroom without incident.

The *go to your room* intervention must be applied with the knowledge that it is likely to fail at some point during the early going. Parents must understand that childhood is a period of testing the limits of parental authority as well as testing the degree of the child's power over the parent. The very early stages of this intervention are likely to result in a great deal of resistance because it represents another form of separation between the child and the parent. This is especially difficult for the child, in that this separation is initiated by the parent, and it is clear that when a child is already angry, more impositions upon the child will not be welcome.

Many parents complain that sending a child to the bedroom is not much of a punishment if the room is loaded with toys, books, TV, and more. This complaint represents two major mistakes that many modern parents are prone to make. First, that a child must experience hurt (see *Motivation, Consequence, and Punishment,* page 126) in order to learn to avoid a behavioral problem; and second (in some ways more harmful) the belief that a child is entitled to such things as TVs, stereos, CD players, video games, and the like (these things are luxuries and should be considered privileges in the child's early life).

Parents must realize that everything in a young child's room has been provided by the parent. Many parents try to compensate for their own difficult childhoods by giving their children everything they did not have as children. A strong, flexible character does not result from being indulged, but rather from hard work, endurance of natural pain, and acceptance of personal responsibility.

A child's bedroom is the place where a child is to sleep, entertain himself, seek refuge against the world, and cool off. The amount of "stuff" that a child is permitted to have in his room should depend upon the child's willingness and ability to accept the responsibility for having that "stuff." If a child cannot go into his bedroom and refrain from turning on a television at the request of the parent, then the television should be removed until such maturity is achieved. If the child cannot, at the parent's direction, go to his room and sit quietly on the bed without doing anything else, then that child will need to learn to do that very thing, and it is the parent's job to teach him (the purpose of *Dynamics*).

Many children who are sent to their rooms grudging comply; they grumble, yell, cry, complain, stomp their feet, and slam the door. As difficult as it may seem, it is important that a parent refrain from making an issue of such things, particularly in the heat of the moment. Most often, the noise that a child makes when complying with a parent's authority is an invitation for the parent to get angry and involved in a chaotic power struggle which often leads to parental guilt. When a child slams a door, that child is driving home the point that she has accepted the imposition, but needs to "save face" by emphatically setting a boundary against the parent. Doors will slam far less often, and nastiness will occur on a far less frequent basis, if parents learn not to bite on their children's invitations to fight while yielding to a parent's ultimate authority.

HOLDING

The last stand that a parent must take while teaching the young child to adhere to parental authority will be the use of *holdings* and physical restraints. Many strong-willed children will test parents to the very edge of their abilities to handle difficult situations (and sometimes beyond), and this is the primary reason that effective parent education, rooted in the realities of human nature, is required for healthy development. As was noted in Chapter 3, a parent must know how to tame a child who is prone to rage (refer to *Holdings and Restraints,* page 143 for the differences between holdings and restraints). When holdings and restraints are employed with parental temperance and compassion, the child learns to let go of rage without harming others and will learn over the long-term to control his inner turmoil with self-restraint and maturity. Holdings and therapeutic restraints are also the best methods for teaching a child that the parent is the ultimate authority in his life and will help set the stage for the success of other less intrusive behavioral interventions.

CAUTIONS

It is extremely important that a parent learns to hold and restrain a child in a healthy, non-coercive, and non-abusive manner. Any parent who is interested in learning more about effective holdings can refer to Martha Welch's book, *Holding Time;* any parent interested in learning to effectively restrain an angry or acting-out child should consult a therapist who is well versed in the theory and application of therapeutic restraint. The essential elements of holding and restraint are as follows (see also pages 143-147):

- Don't use either procedure as an effort to coerce a child to perform some task she does not want to do.
- Holdings are usually done on a schedule (as recommended by Welch).
- Restraints are employed when a child is going out of control.
- A parent must be have the confidence to see a holding or a restraint to its natural conclusion (i.e., a truly calm child)
- A parent must be able to remain calm and emotionally available to the child throughout the processes.

The very best way to employ successful and effective holdings and restraints is to get professional assistance in the early going. When effectively employed, the positive effects of these methods of interacting with a child far outperform the results of any type of punishment (i.e., spanking, yelling, "guilting," threatening, criticizing, and/ or belittling).

TYING THEM TOGETHER: TIME-OUT, GO TO YOUR ROOM, AND HOLDING

The following vignette is a compilation of actual experiences encountered by parents in difficult situations. Although the situation is fictitious, it shows how time-out, go to your room, and holding can be used in concert with one another to effectively address a very serious problem between a child and her parent. Following the vignette is a detailed analysis of how the principles of *Dynamics* work together to engineer the magic of character formation in the midst of what appears to be the worst of circumstances.

> Daphne and her father are together again on a Saturday morning. Dad awakens her at nine o'clock and once again she refuses to get out of bed. As before, he lets her sleep instead of fighting with her to get up. She gets out of bed about an hour later, and she announces that she is starving. Dad tells her that she can have either cereal or eggs for breakfast. Daphne tells her dad that she wants pancakes; he tells her there is no pancake mix and she'll just have to make another choice. She insists that she wants pancakes and tells her dad to go to store. Dad says he's not going to make a special trip to store.
>
> She gets frustrated with her dad and escalates her insistence that she wants pancakes. He tells her she can have eggs or cereal. She then tells her dad that instead of pancakes she wants a toaster pastry; dad tells her there is none in the house. She gets furious and becomes disrespectful. She tells him that he is too stupid to know how to make pancakes from scratch, and that he is a poor shopper because he did not buy enough toaster pastries on his last trip to the store.
>
> Dad has now had enough. He tells Daphne that she has lost the privilege to eat anything at the moment and that she will have to go to her room. She becomes defiant and tells him that she's not going to do anything for such a mean man. Dad insists that Daphne go to her room; she refuses. He tells her that if she does not go to her room under her own power, he will have to escort her there, saying that it's her choice. She makes

a face at him, sticks out her tongue and taunts him with little body gestures that say "make me."

Dad walks toward Daphne; she runs to her room. He continues walking toward her, but slower than she is running; when Daphne gets into her room, she slams the door and locks it. Dad tells her through the door that she is to stay in her room for one half hour. Soon after telling her this, dad makes his way back to the dining room where he starts working on the daily crossword.

A few minutes later dad looks up to see Daphne standing defiantly, glaring at him, almost daring him to get angry and do something bad to her. Dad tells her to go back to her room and stay there for half an hour. She glares. He reiterates that she needs to go to room peacefully or he will have to put his hands on her and help her to the room. She glares.

Dad gets up from his puzzle and moves toward Daphne; this time she does not run; she stands fast. Dad firmly but gently puts his hands on her upper arms and turns her toward her bedroom. Daphne huffs; she puffs, and she physically resists his effort; he attempts to usher her to the room. She digs in her heels and escalates her resistance. Dad very carefully picks her up and takes her into her room.

Once there he closes the door behind him and tells Daphne that she is going to stay in her room and that he will remain there in front of the door to insure that she does not leave again. She tells him to get out. He tells his daughter that he will be glad to leave if she agrees to stay there for the half-hour. She refuses. He stays. She attempts to push past him.

Dad carefully takes her by the arms and moves her to the floor and places her in a basket hold, which he learned from a therapist; he has her arms firmly held against her chest, and has his legs over her legs so that she cannot move. He tells her that he is going to stay with her until she is calm.

Dad holds tightly and tells her to go ahead and get angry, but he also tells her that he is not going to let go until she is calm. Daphne continues to scream that she hates him and that he is killing her. She threatens that she is going to call the police and that he had better let her go or she is going to blow him up when she grows up. He holds on to her and tells her that he loves her and that he will let her go when she is calm, but he repeats that she needs to get her anger out.

Daphne bargains, complains, chides, and promises she will do anything if he will just let her go. Dad holds on, tells her again that he loves her, but he is not going to let go until he is convinced that she is finished with her anger. After about twenty minutes Daphne starts to soften; dad tells Daphne that he loves her and that she is a good girl. She starts to cry.

Daphne tells her dad that she is a bad girl and that she can't understand why he would love such a rotten kid; he assures her that it's okay for a girl to have bouts of rage when growing up. She hugs her dad and kisses him on the cheek. He squeezes her back and kisses her as well.

After a few minutes, Daphne asks dad if she can get a drink of water; dad says he'll get it for her. He returns with the water and tells her that he loves her very much, but she will have to remain in her room for the next one-half hour. She agrees and gives her dad another kiss before he goes back to his puzzle. Her half-hour passes, and for the rest of the day as well as the entire next week, Daphne seems like an all new child: cooperative, friendly, and well mannered.

ANALYSIS

It is clear from the above story that dad did a great deal of work with Daphne on that Saturday morning and it is clear that his daughter made noteworthy emotional strides as a result of his hard work. Dad's efforts were primarily focused upon containing his willful child and trusting that the outcome of this containment would be a calmer, softer, more pliable child. Within his efforts, he employed many of the principles discussed in *Dynamics*.

Principle 1 (unconditional love) was exercised throughout all of dad responses to Daphne's behaviors. Principle 3 (controlling the environment instead of the child) was exercised several ways:

- Dad set the parameters of what could be eaten for breakfast.
- He determined what he would and would not do for Daphne.
- When Daphne went out of control, Dad limited his efforts to containment instead of trying to make her stop raging. In fact, he encouraged her rage, but maintained his control over the environment (i.e., the holding environment).

Principle 4 (No means No) was employed when dad refused to go to the store at Daphne's command, and when he denied her the toaster pastries. Dad also employed this principle during the holding when he refused to yield to Daphne's attempts to bait and bargain with him in her efforts to get free of his grasp.

Principle 6 (being the confident parent) was useful in helping dad get through the very difficult holding period and helping him to steel himself against his daughter's put-downs. The more faith he displayed to Daphne in his ability to contain her, the easier he made it for Daphne to choose to calm down.

Principle 7 (anger is the fire that fuels the character) was evidenced throughout the situation in that Daphne raged throughout the experience. She fell back on her old ally, anger, and employed it to the fullest.

Dad demonstrated an awareness of Principle 9 (refrain from shaming); Principle 10 (temperance is learned by example) in that he was able to maintain an even temper with Daphne throughout her every attempt to gain power over him; and Principle 11 (power at any cost) such that he was able to see through her name-calling and protests as ways to gain the upper hand in the exchange.

Finally, Principle 15 (children must win) was heeded when dad "served" Daphne the glass of water. He was letting her know that he was going to adhere to his dictum regarding restriction to her room, but was willing to demonstrate his love to her on a level that she could understand and take in. Dad was also careful to not give up on Daphne once he started the restraint (Principle 18); Daphne could feel like a winner even though she chose to give in because dad did not give up on loving her throughout the experience.

Dad worked his way through the holding in a manner that showed Daphne he was going to remain with her as long as necessary, because to give up on her would mean sacrificing all of the hard work that he had done up to the point where he quit. To quit would have undoubtedly rendered him even more powerless in the future and would have violated one of the most important principles of powerful parenting: Principle 18 (the parent must not be defeated by the child).

Containment, although often a difficult experience for both parent and child, will yield a child who has the ability to experience sadness, guilt, and remorse in the wake of out-of-control behaviors.

CONTAINMENTS FOR OLDER, LARGER CHILDREN

Once a youngster nears puberty and has passed the sixty pound mark, parents find that physical containment becomes progressively more difficult. In most cases whenever holdings and restraints are employed throughout childhood (from about 4 to 10 years of age) the child will gradually soften his character to allow for flexibility and acceptance of parental authority. By the time adolescence arrives, the child has learned that his parents are reasonable people, flexible yet firm disciplinarians, and trustworthy authority figures. In other words, the young person will have developed sufficient character to no longer require containment for rage and anger because those elements of the child's psyche will have been tamed. In cases when the child does get angry, the child's ability and desire to cope with the feeling will be stronger than the feeling itself. It is important to remember that temper tantrums are a part of childhood, as much as diapers are. Kids will grow out of both as long as the parent doesn't make a big deal about them.

Often, however, it is not until puberty that many parents recognize problems within the parent-child system and it may even be later before the parents seek help. When a child has been raised without adequate limits, boundaries and expectations, or when a child has been parented with a great deal of anger or coercion, there will be an uprising of anger and resistance when the child reaches adolescence. This anger and resistance must be met with reasonable responses (i.e., adequate therapeutic interventions) or there will be a much-increased chance of long-lasting damage for the child.

PARENTAL EFFORTS AT CONTAINMENT: "YOU'RE GROUNDED!"

One of the most common containments for a youngster after early childhood is restriction in the form of a "grounding." However, this tool is often overused as a punishment for multitude of infractions for which there are other more effective interventions. There is a very clear difference between using restrictions for punishment versus using them for containment. When this difference is understood, the parent can use restrictions in a far more effective manner.

Containment is a parent's effort at limiting a child's ability to experience freedom when a young person is going out of control. Punishment, on the other hand, is an effort on the part of the parent to apply a one-time "mega" response to a youngster's behavior that will extinguish that behavior once and for all. The purpose for containment (in this case restriction) is to give the child time to cool down to the point where the child is safe from her desire to inflict destruction upon property, others, and/or self. The purpose of punishment is to teach the child that the parent has absolute control over the child's behavior. In most cases, containments can be used in concert with the win/win philosophy; punishments cannot. When win/win is incorporated into the process of containment, the youngster has control over the amount of time it takes for the containment effort to be successful. Punishment removes the young person's ability to control her own destiny and will therefore bring forth hopelessness and despair. Consider the following:

> Petulant Pete (aged 13) has been having a particularly difficult Saturday morning. He wants to go skateboarding with his friends, but his mother has made it known that he must clean the garage before leaving. He starts to clean the garage, but along the way he picks a fight with his mother (in an effort to get her to say "I don't care what you do, get away from me") and starts being especially demeaning to her. He calls her a few choice names, taunting her to get her angry.
>
> Mom knows this game; Pete has tried this with her in the past and she is ready for his ploy. Immediately after Pete gets loud and obnoxious she informs him that he is grounded to his room. In the past she used to tell him that he's grounded for the day, but this time she tells him he is grounded, period. He asks, "How long?" and she tells him that he is grounded until he decides to clean the garage without arguing with her.
>
> Pete now goes to his room because he knows that if he does not, his mother will call the police to file an unruly charge against him. She's not going to call them to get him to clean his room, but to simply impress upon him the fact that he does not have the choice to refuse to be restricted to his room. Mother taught this lesson to Pete last year after starting his therapy.
>
> Pete stays in his room about fifteen minutes when he starts to think about his situation. He realizes that it will take about thirty minutes to get the garage swept and straightened out, and then he can leave. He calls to his mother (in a noticeably conciliatory tone) that he is ready to get the work done. Also, because he is not as angry as he was earlier, he apologizes to his mother for being so mean to her.

THE LAW

The odds that a child will somehow get involved with the Juvenile Justice System are greatly diminished by following the strategies in this book from as early in a child's life as possible. The longer parents use anger, guilt, control and coercion as their primary means for obtaining and maintaining order within the family, or the longer a parent ignores the disciplinary needs of a child, the greater the chances of legal involvement.

Many parents want to avoid having to deal with the law as far as their children are concerned in that they don't want to get the child into trouble. The mere fact that a parent will take steps to avoid getting the police involved in situations which clearly warrant such will only serve to promote a greater risk of escalating negative behaviors.

Parents who use win/win strategies and reasonable containments will probably never have to contend with any aspects of the law; but parents who get started late and realize they must change their parenting habits, will often find that they will be pushed to this limit by their child to see if the parent will indeed "call the law." As implied in the above sketch, Petulant Pete had already learned that if he pushed his mother too far, she would indeed get the police involved.

A parent should never threaten to call the police unless she will actually follow through with this promise, nor should a parent make threats about having the police take her away for being bad. The primary goal for calling the police out to the home is to file a formal charge (e.g., unruly, domestic violence, or physical abuse against a sibling). What the police do about the situation will be at their discretion and is not nearly as important as the fact that the parent was willing to call them out in the first place.

It must be remembered that all transactions of this nature between a parent and a child are contractual and therefore it is imperative that the parent makes a contract that can be enforced. The promise to file a charge can be broken only if the parent changes his mind. If the parent makes empty threats or promises certain things will happen that don't happen (e.g., "the police will lock you up"), the child learns that both the parent and the Juvenile Justice System are untrustworthy.

There is nothing wrong, however, with the young person conjuring up visions in his mind of being jailed or carted off in handcuffs; there is some likelihood that these fears may help to alter behavior, but it is important that the parent remember to avoid threats in order to gain control over a child. A parent should avoid trying to scare a youngster into submission; at some point he will test the parent and this could lead to unwanted and sometimes disastrous consequences.

Most of the time the need for police intervention with a given child is an indication of a need for a father. This notion can be especially difficult for a father to accept, especially when he feels that he has tried everything to prevent that outcome. In most cases in which the police do get involved, it is almost certain that the father is either too lax in his application of limits and boundaries or he is much too dictatorial in his approach to discipline, or a combination of both.

Similarly, when there is no father in the home and the mother has never learned how to set and maintain limits, the child misses the presence of a strong paternal figure in his life. Many strong-willed children continually test a vunerable mother who may succumb to the test, leaving the child to his own designs. Sometimes society (in the form of the police and judicial system) has to step in to compensate for the mother's inability to assert her authority and the absence of a father.

When a child, any child, exceeds the limits of accepted societal behaviors (e.g., violence or wanton destruction of property) the police should be called immediately and a complaint should be levied. Parents who refrain from doing so find themselves dealing with much greater difficulties later; parents who are willing to do so most often find that the police never need to be called.

SOMETHING TO AVOID WITH AUTHORITIES

Many times when parents bring their children before the court for being unruly or when they accompany their child to some school disciplinary event, something very strange happens. The magistrate, teacher, or school principal will, after going through a variety of options for dealing with the child's behavior, turn to the parent and ask the parent which option she prefers.

This situation occurs more often than one might imagine and tends to put the parent in a very bad spot. Parents of difficult children, as much as they may say otherwise, want someone to take control of the situation with the youngster and bring it under control. So when the magistrate or principal gives the choice of penalty to a parent, the parent is then stuck with having to choose the "best" option.

Whatever choice the parent might make, the parent loses. The child will either learn that the parent is soft and can be manipulated, or feel that the parent is overly punitive and responsible for the bad outcome of the situation. It should be remembered that one of the reasons that children end up in front of an outside authority is because the parent or parents do not know how to deal with issues of power and authority. Asking the parents to make the decision regarding punishment defies reason in that, if the parent knew what to do, the youngster probably wouldn't be in trouble in the first place.

A parent should always defer the decision back to the authority at hand. The parent should never fight for leniency, nor should the parent strive to make sure the punishment is severe enough to teach her a lesson. When a child ends up before an authority external to the family, the parent or parents should be present to be sure that the child is not being abused or railroaded, and should trust the authority to act in the best interest of the child. The parent then can support that decision in the home.

A parent should always be mindful of a child's (especially a willful child's) need to attain power (Principle 11) in a stressful situation in order to ward off the very strong feelings of shame and guilt for not being good enough or not being the perfect child. Parents should also be aware that the further a child is from being perfect, the more shame and guilt that child is likely to feel, and the more power he will crave; often this means the child will act-out to a greater degree and a negative spiral will be set into motion. Parents should work in concert with one another to allow for outside authorities to have their due, thus reducing the power held by the child in the situation, and demonstrate their own respect for social authority to the child.

On the other hand, when a young person comes before an authority figure other than his parent and is summarily disciplined for whatever infraction has been perpetrated, the parent can be supportive of the youngster's feelings about the situation. A parent should remember that the bad thing that happened did in fact happen to the child, and not to the parent. Parents must avoid taking their children's mistakes as personal insults and keep the onus for the mistake on the child. This frees the parent to remain supportive and emotionally present to assist the young person through the bad patch, and thus soothe the emotional situation as time passes.

BAD PLACES: CONTAINMENT ON THE BRINK OF DISASTER

Relationships tend to proceed in cycles; sometimes up, sometimes down; sometimes pleasant and sometimes very difficult. A bad place in a relationship is where both parties of the relationship are unable to contain their bad feelings about a particular matter and some sort of fight breaks out. A bad place in a parenting relationship often occurs when a parent's character is under a great deal of stress and is vulnerable to any perceived rejection, slight, or attack from another; it sometimes happens that the child is that other. Many children (particularly the strong-willed) are often insensitive to the needs of a parent who is emotionally out of sorts, and will tend to join with the parent's negativity instead of avoiding or soothing that negativity. Therefore, rather than being tolerant and mindful of the parent's bad feelings, the youngster will act to exacerbate the situation by deliberately pushing the parent beyond his or her level of tolerance. The child will actually work to get the parent to lose her temper, even at the risk of emotional or physical self-injury (Principle 11).

PRINCIPLE 20

> *Bad places exist in nearly all relationships because bad places exist within all people. In the parent-child relationship, you must make sure that all visits to bad places are initiated by and limited to your child's internal world. Don't compound your child's bad places with your own.*

Why would a child deliberately prod a parent to the point of distraction, only to suffer the wrath of that angry parent?

Because he can, and he must.

HE CAN

As noted throughout this book, it is natural for a human being to desire power, and when the parent is at his most vulnerable point, a child (especially the strong-willed child) can be at his peak of power. This process is usually unconscious and is not well thought out by the child, but nonetheless she will often make things worse because the opportunity is there, much like a moth being drawn to a flame.

Often, the child is held accountable for these forays into the land of the parent's psyche, and finds himself on the short end of a very unpleasant experience with the parent. Yet in the end, this truth remains: ongoing visits to bad places in a child-parent relationship are shared experiences between the parent and the child. It is the child who will force his way into them; it is the parent who has the responsibility for leading the way out (by containing her own bad place).

HE MUST

In days long gone, when a parent (especially the father) reached his bad place with a child (i.e. anger), the child would immediately discontinue whatever caused the parent to experience this bad feeling. This was the parenting style of mid-twentieth century when the rules for the family were simple: dad makes them, mom and dad execute them, and the kids follow them. The notion that a bad emotional place within a parent was the fault of the child was the norm. In those days, children made parents angry and they were punished for doing so.

Today's world is different. Changes in the social fabric of our culture force the successful parent to realize that all feelings come from within. In the end a child acts like a child and a parent must act like an adult. A parent gets angry with a child because of the parent's character, not the child's. Modern parents must learn that emotional balance is achieved by learning to master one's own emotions (i.e., internal containment) and to realize that blaming another for inner happenings gives power over to that other.

Children are destined to make attempts to anger and upset a parent because that is what children do. Once the parent gets angry or visibly out of control, the child has succeeded in gaining power over him. The child then takes the parent back to this bad place because the she cannot tolerate the pressure of having power over the parent. As long as the parent continues to lose control, the child will work to repeat the cycle until the parent corrects his or her own inner struggles.

At first, this notion seems to make no sense. It seems that the reverse should be true, that as soon as a child sees the parent go out of control, the child would back off because the threat of an angry parent is terrifying. Part of this assertion is indeed true—the part about the terror. What isn't true is that this terror will stop the child from doing the very thing that created the angry situation with the parent. The psychological need to resolve this terror keeps the child invested in bringing the parent back to the bad place until the parent "gets it right." This same thing often happens in marriage where one spouse will continually repeat annoying behaviors to test the other's patience.

ONCE AGAIN, WHY?

Children need to feel safe. If a parent has a vulnerability (a small crack in his or her character), the child will intuit it; this awareness creates anxiety and a feeling of unease within the child. As a result, some children avoid angering the parent by withdrawing for safety. This in itself should not be considered a good thing due to the fact that any child who withdraws out of fear is likely to later aggravate a parent by passive-aggressive (sneaky or unseen, yet felt) means. On the other hand, a more aggressively inclined child works at widening that crack with more visible methods.

All the while a child is working on the parent, the parent is defending against revealing his or her vulnerability to the child by way of denial, rationalization, and/or blame. Ultimately anger and threats of punishment are employed to bring the child in line. When the child eventually relents (usually due to fear of physical harm), the parent is tempted to nurture the illusion that he has restored control by way of angering, threatening and punishing—in other words, by losing self-control. These types of parenting strategies lead to long-term resentments and eventual difficulties later in theadult child's experiences of intimacy.

The anxiety of the child in relationship to a parent's bad place mounts as the parent becomes more and more out of sorts. A good example of this dynamic is racism. At a very early age the child, may sense her parent's racial biases and begin to ask questions. As the parent explains, rationalizes, or denies the subject matter, the child asks more questions. If these questions put the parent on the spot, the parent may well increase her defensiveness and thus increase the child's anxiety in the child-parent relationship on the matter of racism. The child works ever harder to get to the root of the parent's attitudes and the parent escalates the defensiveness. This can take years to unfold, but eventually this process of escalation can result in a blow-up between the parent and the child.

Such a blow up might occur one morning after a sermon in church about tolerance; perhaps after the child receives formal education on the matter in school; or when he dates someone outside of his own race in adolescence. Whenever it occurs, this blow up becomes a bad place in the parent-child relationship, testing the parent's love. When at such a bad place, the child feels that the parent has sacrificed the bond they share to prevent the revelation and acceptance of an undesirable character trait. This then leads to two character flaws that become secondary to that of racism: hypocrisy and denial of the parent's true self.

Once the youngster knows that something is definitely the matter with the parent on this particular issue (i.e., race), she will take the parent back to this bad place in an unconscious effort to get the parent to resolve the matter in a reasonable manner (and to get the parent's ultimate approval). If the parent does not reach the point within herself where she can handle the matter without losing control, the bad place can remain throughout the lifetime of the relationship. Other examples of parental bad places are attitudes about poor school grades, wearing makeup, dating, driving, religion, politics, alcohol usage, defiance, and more.

Bad places are almost always an indication that the parent has not yet fully emotionally matured. When considering bad places, it is the parent's job to mature, not the child's. The fact is, a child will grow up naturally, as long as the parent has the wherewithal to demonstrate maturity by adequately coping with her own bad places.

If a parent is not able to successfully cope with weaknesses in his character, it will be extremely difficult for the child to get past the place where he is stuck with the parent. When the parent does not work to strengthen his own character, the child is more than likely to learn to handle sensitive issues in the same manner as modeled by the parent. The youngster then has to learn to resolve the very same bad places when his own adulthood is reached. There is a strong likelihood that without the effects of some life changing event, the cycle of going to bad places will continue as the child ages, marries and starts a family. Simply put, when a person learns to handle his bad places, he is ready to successfully share the many benefits (and disappointments) of life with other people.

SUMMARY

Containment is actually about three intimately related experiences. It is about a parent's efforts to prevent a child from getting too far outside of acceptable limits for freedom; a parent's ability to maintain outward behavioral control in spite of her inner world emotional experiences in relationship to the wayward child; and a parent's ability to protect the integrity of the parent-child bond. When a parent learns to combine firmness with empathy, the good enough parent witnesses ongoing growth and maturity in the child and within himself. A parent's ability to successfully handle the bad places that exist for both the parent and the child offers a significantly improved chance for successful emotional and intimate relationships throughout life.

Worksheet

CONTAINMENT REVISITED

1. What is the difference between holding (and/or restraint) and coercion?

2. Should a parent hold a small child who refuses to comply with requests and tasks? Why?

3. What is the difference between a limit and a boundary?

4. What is empathy?

5. When applying a time-out, should the parent keep adding more time if the child refuses to comply with the time-out demand? Why or why not?

6. Do you agree that a child should be permitted to slam the bedroom door when sent there for containment? Why or why not?

7. When holding a child, should a parent hold the child tightly enough to cause pain in an effort to make the situation uncomfortable, thus providing motivation for the child to relent? Explain.

8. If you are the parent of a problem child, when did you first recognize the problem? What was your method for dealing with the child?

9. If you have sought professional assistance for help with your child, how long after you recognized the problem did you wait to get help? Why?

10. Would you be willing to support your child's school teachers and administration if your child got into trouble at school?

11. Would you know how to be empathetic with your child while supporting the school in some problem situation?

12. Would you be willing to call the police and file a complaint if your child became physically threatening? How about if she left home while restricted? If you found drugs and or alcohol in your child's room?

13. On a scale of 1 to 10 (ten being perfect) how well do you handle anger when things don't go your way?

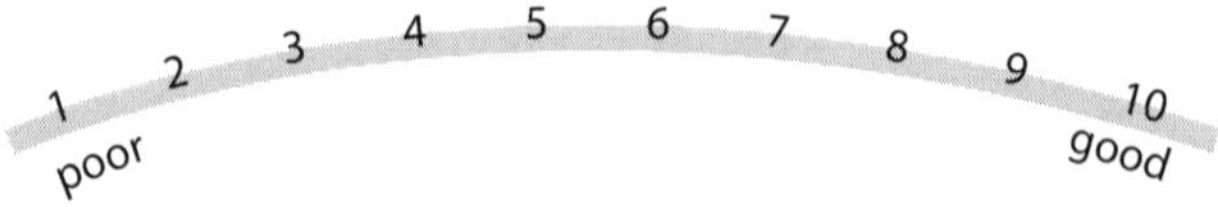

14. On a scale of 1 to 10 how well do you handle anger when things with people don't go your way?

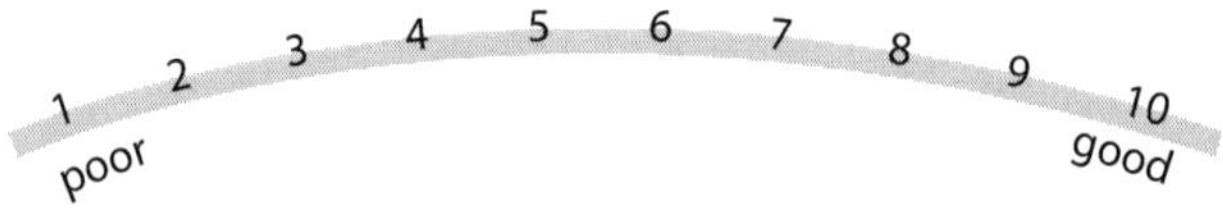

15. On a scale of 1 to 10 how well do you handle anger when your child is angry with you?

16. What is the softest spot in your character? How is this soft spot played out in your relationship with your child? Describe a bad place for you and one of your children.

7

RELATIONSHIPS

PRINCIPLE 21

> *A pure, healthy relationship is one in which each person can be true to himself with no fear, pretense or forced deference. When this occurs between parent and offspring, one of life's greatest joys is experienced. Further, when this relationship does exist, it will likely be modeled later in life within the adult child's new family.*
>
> *Love is one thing, but true joy exists between a parent and child who really like each other to the point that they enjoy one another's company.*

Relationships are products of parenting experiences. Children who are parented with love, stability, trust, discipline, and dignity are likely to enter into similar relationships as adults. The same will be true for children who are parented with anger, disdain, competition, criticism, disrespect, instability, and mistrust; they will likely find their lives filled with more of the same. There are exceptions to be sure, and we hear or read about them from time to time. "Good" parents sometimes raise a "bad" child, and "good" people sometimes emerge from "bad" parenting. Yet on the whole, the better the job of parenting, the better the chances for a psychologically healthy person and satisfactory relationships in adulthood.

As noted throughout *Dynamics,* parenting is a process that unfolds throughout the lifetime of every person. This process creates the groundwork for all future relationships as well as the relationship that will exist between the grown-up child and her own children. The quality of parenting greatly influences the quality of parenting given in the next generation.

What follows is a model for understanding and viewing the growth of a child in relationship with the parent. This model is not exact nor is it intended to be so. It will present certain claims which are clearly arguable, yet in the end, the conceptualizations that emerge can be valid and helpful for a better understanding of relationships.

THE BASICS

To understand the process of parenting across the spectrum of childhood, a few basics need to be put in place.

Mothering: the First Relationship

Mothering, simply defined, is the total devotion of the mother (or mother substitute) to the welfare of her baby. There are no questions about limits, boundaries, discipline, or unacceptable behaviors. Everything about mothering is virtually one-sided. Mothering rarely lasts more than the first year of a child's life. If it did, the mother would be sorely taxed and would require a major ongoing adjustment to her own expectations for life. Consider the mother of a child with a serious debilitating illness. The amount of mothering required in such a situation is overwhelming, yet many women, as well as men, must and do yield to these demands daily.

Mothering in most cases should be employed at a rate of one hundred percent throughout the first year of a child's life. After the first year, as the child reaches toddlerhood, mother must learn to slowly give up mothering in favor of becoming a parent.

It should be noted here that, although the term mothering is being used to describe the process of complete indulgence, this process must not be limited strictly to mothers. The father can and must be responsible for mothering as the father-child relationship develops, particularly in infancy. It is extremely important that father learns to demonstrate his presence in each of the three parent-child realms presented here.

Parenting: the Second Relationship

As the infant passes into toddlerhood, mothering must give way to parenting. Different from mothering, parenting is the process of applying limits and consequences to the child at various times to instruct the child to adopt acceptable behaviors; it is the business of molding, shaping, programming, and directing a child's development. This is what much of *Dynamics* is all about.

The change from mothering to parenting is slow, but in time the child should be given limits to which to adhere, and various parenting methods must be employed to impose those limits. The child must learn to conduct herself in an acceptable manner by way of the parent's efforts throughout childhood; this education is the job of parenting...not of mothering. Mothering is the process of indulging and satisfying the child's every want and need without limits; this practice must gradually decrease, lest the child become spoiled. Mothering and parenting are performed by both parents; however, mothers are usually better at mothering while fathers are often more adept at parenting; this is one reason that many fathers become more active in a child's life as the child grows older.

Many mothers are not familiar with the difference between mothering and parenting, and often fall victim to their own efforts to be a "good" mother (this happens to a lesser extent with fathers). It is unfortunate that there is not more thought given to being a "good" parent, because a "good" parent strives to teach responsibility (which is not learned by way of an indulgent relationship). On the other hand, fathers often go too far toward the "good" father aspect of interacting by becoming too strict and demanding. As a result many fathers need to learn to be better at mothering and interactive relating (see below).

Interactive Relating: the Third Relationship

Interactive relating (referred to as "relating") is the act of being oneself with another. As mothering slowly dwindles, parenting increases, and the child begins to exist within the limits of a safe world. This safety allows for the person of the child to develop. This development is internal to the child, but does not take place in a vacuum. The child as a person begins to seek contact with the parent, and the parent connects with the child; not just for needs gratification, limiting and instructing, but rather for the simple joy of relating. The child and the parent talk, play, and mutually interact with one another. At first, in infancy and early childhood, it seems that the child is totally self-absorbed and often does little else besides ask questions, but gradually, over time, the child begins to synthesize his own thoughts and ideas, and shares them with mother and/or father.

By the time a child reaches the age of five years, mothering should be about fifty percent of the relationship, parenting about thirty percent, and relational interacting approximately twenty (see graph below). Naturally, these percentages are approximations and will vary from one parenting situation to another, but generally speaking, they are relatively representative of what is happening in the parent-child relationship.

Developmental Shifts in Relational Priorities

Figure 1 gives a pictorial representation of the above summarization of the three interactive modes of relating with a child. It also gives the reader an idea of how the priorities of the parent-child relationship tend to shift throughout childhood.

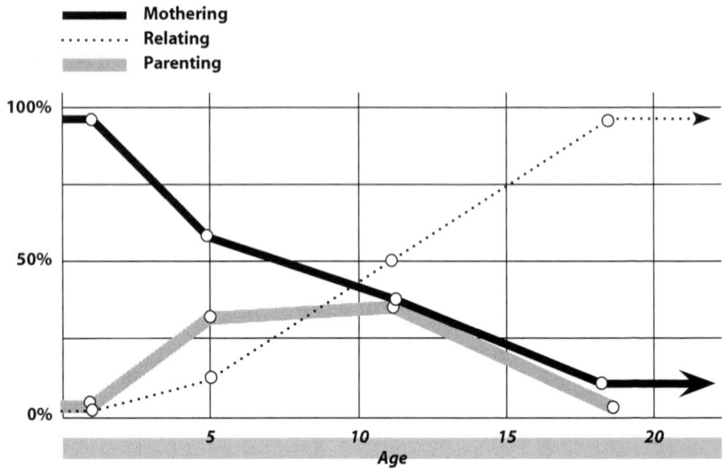

Fig. 1 *Relational Grid*

Notice that during the first year, the entire relationship is devoted to mothering. As the child develops, the percentages begin to change. By the time age five is reached, parenting is still outranked by mothering, but the trend is clear: parenting and relating are taking over. When adolescence sets in (near age twelve), mothering is typically greatly diminished, parenting is peaking, relating on the rise.

PRINCIPLE 22

By the time a child reaches adolescence, what a parent does is not nearly as important as what has already been done.

A grave mistake is made by many parents who try to continue to parent an adolescent as though the adolescent were only eight or nine years old.

By the time adolescence arrives, parents need to realize that the bulk of the parenting should have already been accomplished and further attempts to guide and direct the child will result in numerous (and most of the time, useless) power struggles. A parent must learn to trust the job he has done with the child during early and middle childhood, and learn to let the child make her own mistakes from which to learn life's lessons (especially as adolescence progresses).

It is interesting to note that the graph shows that mothering never really stops, although parenting falls to zero. The reason for this apparent inconsistency is twofold: first, once a child is eighteen years old, it is a forgone conclusion that he is an adult and must be responsible as such. Thus, no parenting need be applied (it will likely be rejected anyway). Second, it is the nature of the human being to always look at offspring as children and for children to continue to see parents as parents. Special occasions (e.g., Christmas, birthdays, holidays) and hard times (e.g., unforeseen financial difficulties) often bring out the mother in a parent, and the child in an adult. This is an okay thing, for it allows the adult child to re-experience the essence of childhood and the safety of knowing that there is always someplace for him to go for strength and stability. It is important that the parent of an adult child to recognize that these episodes of mothering are temporary or at best short-lived; for the child must get back to the business of being an adult. There is also the harsh reality that the longer one lives, the closer the death of the parents, and once they are gone, there is no one to take over for them.

PROCESSES

Either/or

Everybody has a predisposition to a certain way of living, to a particular kind of personality. Generally speaking there are two basic temperaments: aggressive and avoidant (passive). People either tend to be outward or inward; there really doesn't seem to be much middle ground. There are various styles of personality, and varying ways of getting what one wants, but in the end there are two basic predispositions for being human: either aggressive or avoidant, dominant or recessive, outward or inward.

Aside from the two styles of personalities for people, there is also the apparent fact that people can opt for either one or the other poles in a given situation. It is possible for a relatively timid person to become aggressive when pushed beyond her limits of tolerance, or for an aggressive person to take on an avoidant stance when he realizes that the situation at hand may be lost. It is important to note, however, that when a person is being aggressive, essentially there is no avoidance; and when a person is being avoidant, there is no outward aggression. The *passive-aggressive* situation, as will be discussed later in this chapter, is an apparent exception to this notion in that the person experiences the desire to inflict pain (aggression) in concert with the fear of doing so openly (avoidance).

Understanding that people have these two basic natures helps us to see why one child can be difficult while another is very easy. Children who are destined to be aggressive are often a handful from toddlerhood and beyond, while children who are basically passive are easy to parent and not much trouble at all throughout much of their development.

When one accepts that people are not locked into being a certain way all the time, the aggressive and avoidant styles can be placed on a continuum (Fig. 2).

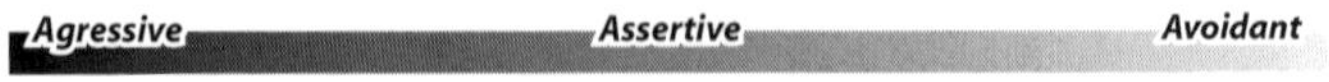

Fig. 2 *Dispositions Continuum*

It is important to note that, although predispositions cannot be changed, the alternate style can be learned (usually by way of tempering—i.e., by way of experiencing and working through painful social and intimate situations). This fact leaves room in the center of the continuum for mixtures of aggressive and avoidant behaviors that can be considered to be assertive (note: assertiveness is defined here as the ability to stand one's ground without giving into the tendency to shrink away with fear or to inflate with anger). Thus, for example, a child who is predisposed to be aggressive might learn to avoid trouble by changing his behavior in daycare, while a shy or timid child might learn to stand up for herself on the playground in elementary school. Thus, the continuum can be looked upon as a range of percentages spanning the 100% aggressive person to the 100% avoidant person; either extreme will produce mental health difficulties unless tempered by the natural forces of life and through the parenting process.

PRINCIPLE 23

Learn to honor the differences between your children, instead of labeling them either good or bad. Children are much more likely to be mentally healthy when they realize that both good and bad elements are a part of themselves.

Splitting

Splitting occurs when a person's view of the world is reduced to good or bad; right or wrong. People who split their world tend to see things in black and white without much room for gray. They tend to be somewhat rigid in their thinking and often present as moody or temperamental, quickly shifting from feeling good about something to feeling very bad about the same thing. Usually this occurs when the perceived object (i.e., person or thing) has somehow betrayed the preconceived notions of the observer.

A simple example of splitting would be the child who makes a new best friend at school and comes home feeling on top of the world, saying the nicest things about this new friend; only to come home the next day cursing that same person because she did not wait to have lunch together. The youngster cannot see that the new best friend can still be a good person even though she doesn't conform to all expectations.

Many adults have a tendency to exercise splitting in their daily lives without noticing, and when splitting is practiced by parents within the family, a variety of ills can result. One example of splitting happens when parents find themselves with two children. Time after time they find these two children to be as different as night and day, and as time passes, one parent takes on the belief that one of the children is good and the other is bad, while the other parent has a tendency to see things in just the opposite way. This type of splitting can start as early as infancy and develop from that point onward. After a time, each of the children will begin to conform to the perceptions of each parent and it is likely that one parent will become aggressive and the other protective. The differences will be revealed in each family member's behaviors. One child will experience power and an inflated sense of self-worth, while the other will experience powerlessness and lowered self-worth; one parent will be the good guy, and the other will be the bad guy. All will cling to their perceptions of one another with unyielding determination and the family will start to come apart at the seams if the situation is not adequately addressed.

The damage that occurs within such a system can be extensive; one child will have a great deal of difficulty accessing his inner negativity, while the other will find it extremely difficult to find the good that is buried within. Unless each parent lets go of strongly held beliefs about the children and each other, the system will remain unhealthy. In the end the children will likely experience difficulty in future intimate relationships, and the parents will remain bitter and unhappy with one another.

Splitting and Triangulation

As noted above, splitting occurs when one person sees others as either good or bad. The phenomena of splitting naturally leads to the existence of triangular relationships in which one party will deem other parties either good or bad, right or wrong, better or lesser. When this triangulation occurs in a family, a variety of results will ensue.

Consider the following example:

> Dominic and Milo are 10 year-old fraternal twins and are the only two children in their family. Dominic tends to be aggressive, outgoing and controlling while Milo tends to be more shy, retiring and dependent. Ever since they were toddlers, Dominic has been the one who chooses all the TV shows, activities and games, and he is the one who routinely gets dibbs on common toys (electronic hand held games, video games, and such) and the front seat of the car when only one parent is on hand.
>
> Milo has been the target of a great deal of Dominic's aggression. Dominic will taunt him, poke at him when no one is looking, make fun of him, and exercise a variety of other mean behaviors designed to overpower his brother.
>
> The twins' parents tend to see Milo as the victim of his brother and have for years stepped in to help protect him from Dominic's aggression. Mother will punish Dominic for being so mean, while dad will chide Milo to buck up and learn to strike back at Dominic. These encouragements from dad often hurt Milo because dad has used such words as wimp or wussie, when trying to "toughen him up."
>
> Nothing attempted by either parent seems to stop the bickering between the two, and the parents find themselves arguing about the right thing to do about the twins' conflicts. Each parent is often embarrassed by the twins' behaviors when the boys are together, and relieved when they are separate. Overall, each parent feels like a failure, and neither can find a solution to the dilemma which will yield peace and harmony to the family.

This sketch represents a situation that many families experience. The triangulation difficulties illustrated are a result of psychological splitting that is unseen by the participants.

There are several triangles at work in this family; only the most obvious will be examined here.

In this triangle Dominic is the aggressor, Milo is the victim, and mother is the rescuer (of Milo), but as soon as mother intervenes the nature of the triangle shifts. When mother rescues Milo, she unwittingly grants a great deal of power to Milo in that he is the cause for Dominic's punishment, and by punishing Dominic, she makes Dominic her victim. Dominic now sees his mother as bad and his brother as more powerful than he. Eventually Dominic will retaliate to regain his position of power over Milo, only to lose it again when the cycle repeats.

If the mother were able to see each of her children as the master of his own world, then she would leave the two to resolve their own problems without stepping in to take over. On those occasions when the boys prove themselves unable to resolve their problems, and the situation escalates out of control, she can step in to respond to the ruckus (noise), and essentially penalize each for contributing to that noise. She must at all costs avoid trying to settle the issue between the two, for that results in choosing sides. When that happens, triangulation again takes over (see *Sibling Rivalry*, page 150 for help on how to intervene in sibling rivalry situations).

Splitting is a very common occurrence in most families and social contexts, yet many parents who do split their children have a tendency to deny that they are doing so, thus hiding this truth from themselves, their children and others. They often state that they love both of their children equally, but usually have a great deal of doubt and hidden anger toward the more oppositional child. Any parent who questions whether she is internally splitting her children need only listen to the children and spouse. The signs are there if only the parent will heed them.

The Relational Continuum

Regardless of predispositions to be either aggressive or avoidant, and of the tendency to exercise splitting, ***parent-child*** relationships exist on a continuum. This relational continuum differs from the continuum for personality styles in that relationships are not either/or, but rather a blend of two extremes (enmeshment and estrangement). There is a great deal of room between the poles of the continuum for a healthy middle ground.

The location of the child-parent relationship on this continuum is dependent upon three criteria: the degree and quality of the parent-child bonding in infancy, the degree and quality of separation in toddlerhood, and the tolerance of differences in the parent-child fit throughout childhood (i.e., the avoidance of splitting).

Fig. 3 *Personality Styles Continuum*

OUTCOMES

Enmeshed Relationships

Enmeshment is the term that describes relationships in which there is very poor boundary definition and where the members of the system tend to form a single emotional being. Some examples of enmeshment behaviors in a family system might be:

- answering questions directed at another
- feeling for another
- finishing another's thought
- overprotecting
- blind obedience
- forced obedience
- child and parent sleeping together on a regular basis
- lack of independent thought

Contrary to what many might think, an enmeshed bond is not healthy. An enmeshed bond is often the result of an overabundance of dependency within the mother-child bond and a great deal of fear that the relationship is at risk unless attended to constantly.

An enmeshed bond usually starts out well formed, but the mother soon begins to act-out her own unresolved separation issues from her childhood as the child reaches toddlerhood and then beyond. The mother is afraid that something terrible will happen to her child if she (the mother) is not constantly available. Therefore, she continually seeks contact with her child; her attitude and her actions tend to give the child the message that he (the child) should not be separate from the mother. Thus, the child is unable to distance from the mother and will absorb mother's fear and anxiety, make it part of the relationship with the mother, act it out with the mother (and others), and ultimately internalize this anxiety as a lack of self-confidence.

Estranged Relationships

Estranged relationships are products of damage that occurs in early infancy and toddlerhood resulting from either a broken or poorly formed connection between the child and the mother. If the mother-child bond is not sought by the mother during infancy, the child-mother bond is less likely to occur for the child. When the child-mother bond fails to form, the child is often unable to experience solid, satisfactory attachments throughout her life.

Calling this estrangement a "relationship" is almost a contradiction in terms, with isolation and alienation becoming the behavioral norms for the child (as illustrated in the next section). The truly difficult thing for the child who is lost in an estranged relationship is that she desperately wants to relate with others, but is incapable of knowing how to do so within acceptable means.

Estranged children can be angry or depressed, oppositional or compliant, hostile or avoidant, but no matter what their style, these children will not be able to relate well in intimate relationships. Estranged relationships are most often experienced in foster and adoptive situations.

Healthy Relating and Well-differentiated Relationships (the Middle Ground)

As noted in Chapter 1, psychological attachment occurs in the first year of a child's life, and healthy attachment is absolutely necessary for successful future relationships. Attachments are formed by the continual gratification of an infant's needs in an attitude of mother's love and concern. Initially, mother does all the work in the process, but gradually the child begins to absorb mother's love, as well as her material gifts, and the child then returns love to mother in the form of recognition and desire for her company.

Solid psychological attachment gives way to a need for separation on the part of the child. In some ways this event is paradoxical; just as the bond between child and mother becomes strong, the child begins to move away. It must be noted that the child's distancing is not a threat to the parent-child bond, but rather a reflection of its strength.

With separation comes differentiation (i.e., the understanding that people are separate and different from one another), and that a person who is well-differentiated is neither enmeshed with nor estranged from others. The well-differentiated person has struck a balance between the need to be with others and the desire to be alone.

When successful attachment and separation occur, the relationships between parent and child have the potential to thrive as long as the parents avoid splitting and are mindful of the need to tolerate the differences in personality styles that might exist within the family system.

Putting It Together

Figure 4 (below) illustrates how the aggressive-avoidant and enmeshed-estranged factors fit together.

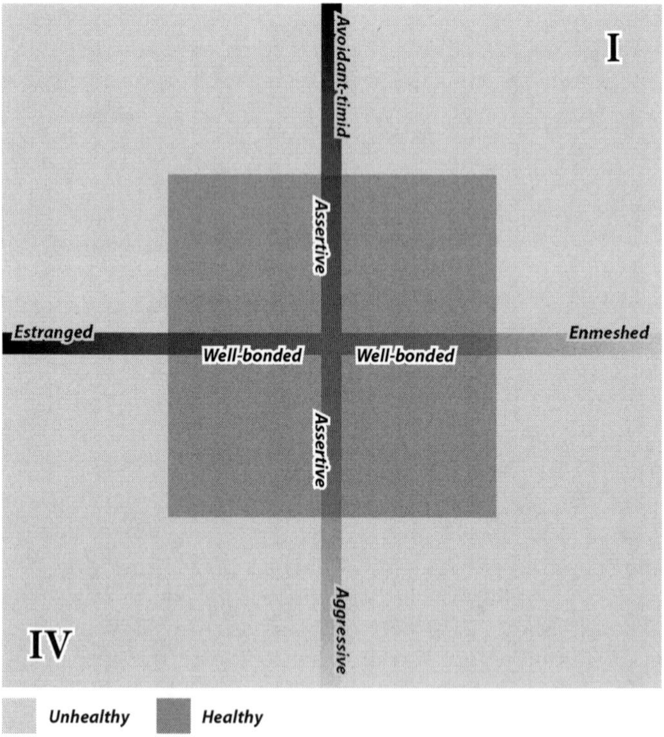

Fig. 4 *Dispositions and Personality Styles Matrix*

Relationship Styles

When considering the four styles of relationships (fig. 4, previous page), it is important to remember that every child-parent relationship fits somewhere on the grid. Just because a relationship falls into a particular category does not mean that it is dysfunctional. Each quadrant of the grid is indicative of the four basic styles of relating. The closer to the center of grid, the healthier the relationship, and the healthier the child/person; the further away from center (particularly in the direction of the aggressive-estranged), the more dysfunctional the relationship, and the more potentially dangerous the child/person.

What follows is an outline of the four basic relationship types. After examining the relationships in the extreme, a model for a healthy parent-child relationship will be presented.

The four styles of relating are represented by four quadrants:

- avoidant-enmeshed (Quadrant I)
- aggressive-enmeshed (Quadrant II)
- avoidant-estranged (Quadrant III)
- aggressive-estranged (Quadrant IV)

Relationship Types

Once the four quadrants of the grid are formed, it is then possible to categorize the relationships as they fit on the overall grid. For example, if a child (boy 1) is relatively outgoing, expressive and well connected to his mother (i.e., assertive and well attached), his location on the grid might appear on the next page (figure 5). If, however, another boy (boy 2) is more enmeshed with his mother and more aggressive than assertive, he would fall into a more dysfunctional portion of the grid as shown.

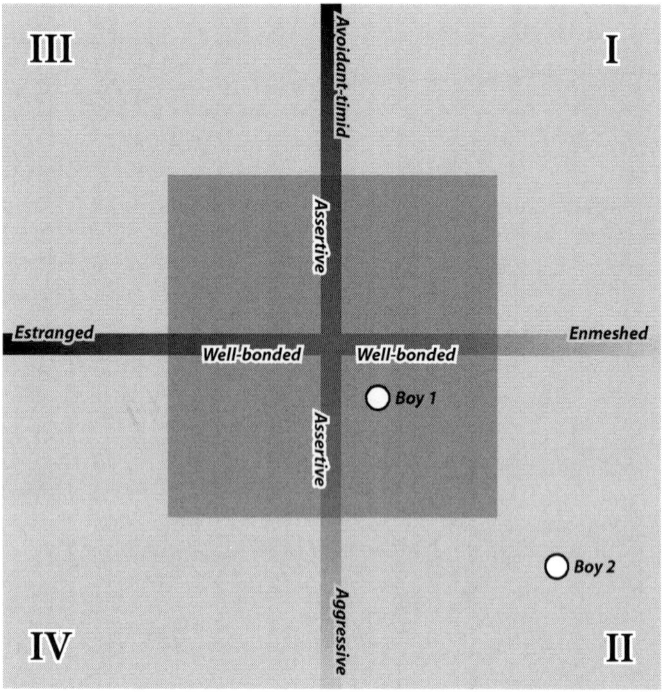

Fig. 5

It can be seen from the graph that a well attached, outgoing boy will fall well within the confines of being an emotionally healthy person; whereas the more enmeshed, aggressive boy falls within the unhealthy range.

It must be remembered that any particular child's placement on the grid will be the result of where she is seen on the dispositional and styles' continua (figures 2 and 3). Objectivity in such matters can be quite difficult to achieve; sometimes it is necessary to get opinions apart from those of the parent or person who is plotting the positions.

Figure 6 (next page) is a graphic representation of various types of personality styles that fall on the grid map. Each style is represented in the extreme within each quadrant to more clearly accentuate the nature of the style in question. The graph is followed by a series of explanations for each of the more pronounced styles in the four quadrants and what can be done to bring these styles back toward a more healthy balance.

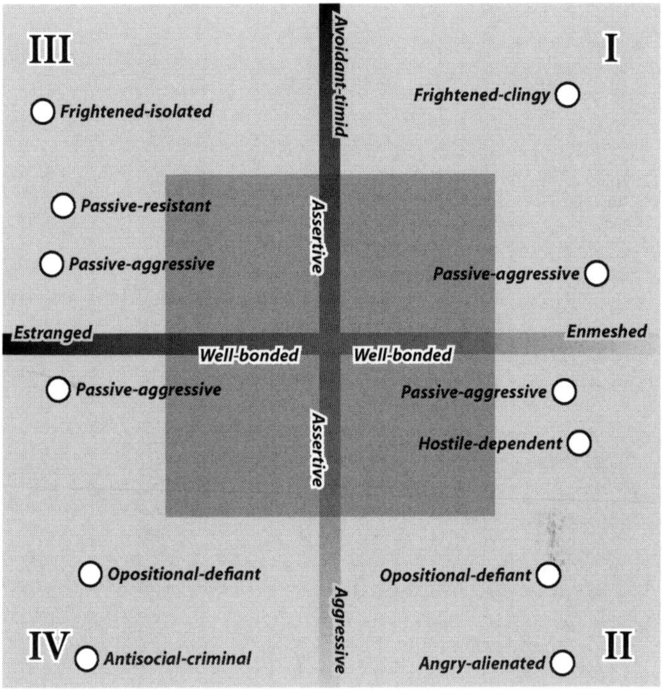

Fig. 6

Avoidant-enmeshed (Quadrant I)

Avoidant-enmeshed situations arise when separation anxiety issues are not successfully resolved by the end of toddlerhood. The avoidant-enmeshed child has a relatively strong bond with the parent which has been compromised by the anxiety that exists between the child and the parent. As noted in chapter 2, the child will likely exhibit clingy behaviors that are a direct result of the fear of losing the parent (and the parent's fear of losing the child). Note: the passive-aggressive style will be examined separately, later.

The frightened-clingy child is the child who simply has a great deal of difficulty with mother's absence. Many of these children have trouble separating at daycare, school, the sitter's, going into rooms alone, and sleeping in their own bedrooms. From early on, there is often a discernible amount of worry about the child's ability to tolerate routine daily challenges.

These children often become a nuisance to their parents, and as the

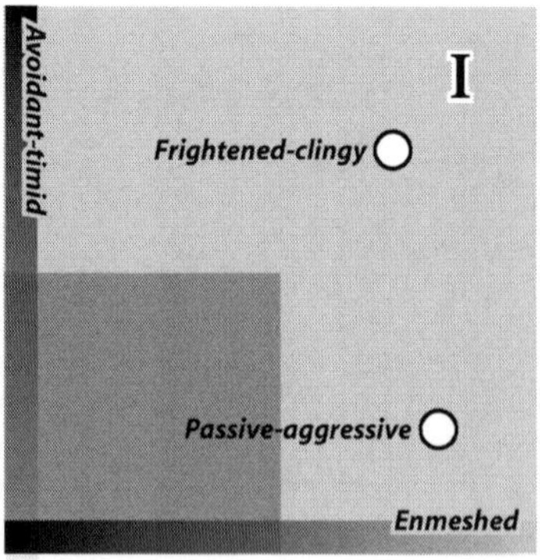

Fig. 7 *Avoidant-enmeshed (Quadrant I)*

child grows, these parents begin to tire of the constant energy drain of the child. There are usually a variety of feelings that beset the mother (and father) with the frightened-clingy child. First, mother may be in denial that there is actually a problem; she may say things like "He's just shy," or "She prefers to be around adults rather than other children," or "We're like Mutt and Jeff, we do everything together." Later, mother or father may become caustic toward the child in an attempt to get the child to separate (e.g., "Why do you always have be under my feet," or "Why can't you do anything on your own?"), or the parents may bicker with one another due to contention over how close is too close. For example, the father may say to the mother, "He wouldn't be like this if you didn't baby him so much."

Some parents will try to push this child to do things he or she does not wish to do, then get angry at the child for balking or failing to perform. These attempts are often unsuccessful for promoting individuality in that the child is threatened by the parent's "rejection," and will then tend to try to move even closer (increase the clinging behaviors). After trying to force a separation with the child, the parent may feel guilty and then resort to indulging the child in some fashion out of pity. This gives the child the message that she can't handle difficult feelings, and at the same time gives power to the child's resistance and helplessness.

The resolution for the frightened-clingy situation is for the parent to recognize the dynamics of the relationship and then allow for emotional (and physical) separation that will result when the parent pulls out of the dependent relationship with the child. Usually this process should be slow and well thought-out due to the child's internalized beliefs of helplessness and terror (of losing the parent). Professional help is a great plus.

Aggressive-enmeshed (Quadrant II)

This quadrant contains the passive-aggressive, hostile-dependent, oppositional-defiant, and angry-alienated personality types. These youngsters have an attachment with the mother and father that goes back to infancy, and are considered to be children who have a conscience, but appear to lack such. The groundwork for these personality types is laid in toddlerhood and remains unresolved due to the parent's overbearing need for control and the failure of the youngster to successfully separate and individuate. The driving emotional force for these personalities is the frustration and eventual anger that results from the inability to be recognized as an individual by the parent(s).

Let's begin with the oppositional-defiant child, the child who continually opposes the parent (or other authority). When the parent says "Yes," the child says "No"; when the parent says "Up," he says "Down"; when the parent says 'Green,' he says "Blue," and so on. This relationship is considered normal for toddlers, but abnormal in later developmental stages. The oppositional-defiant situation can also arise in estranged situations. The enmeshed variation is examined here.

The enmeshed, oppositional-defiant child is often a child who is struggling to separate from the parent, but is not permitted to do so unless wholly on the parent's terms (which in reality creates only an illusion of separation). The parent of the oppositional-defiant child is overly controlling due to an unconscious need to make the child be the ideal child as envisioned in the parent's mind.

The dynamics of this oppositional-defiant system are somewhat paradoxical, in that on the surface the child appears to be separating from

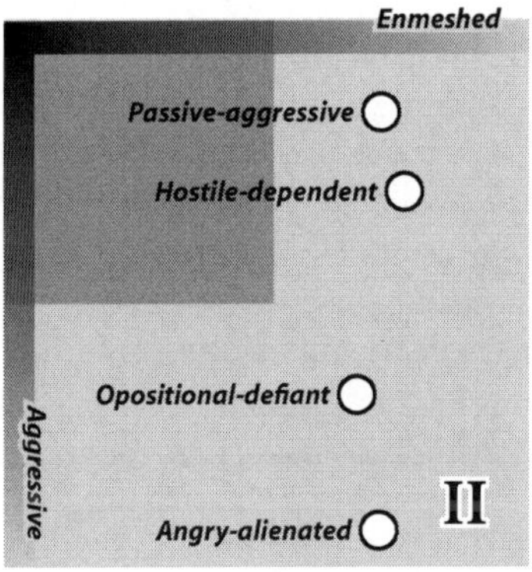

Fig. 8 *Aggressive-enmeshed (Quadrant II)*

the parent (albeit by way of defiance and opposition), while simultaneously experiencing an increase in strong emotion (i.e., anger, fear, and shame) with the parent. This increase in emotionality, although negative, results in a very close and very intense relationship. As this negative closeness increases, the child redoubles her efforts to pull away from the parent (i.e., by escalating oppositional behaviors) and thus increases the level of anger between the two. As this process builds, the parent tries ever harder to "get the child under control," and thus a vicious cycle is created.

The resolution to the enmeshed-oppositional situation is for the parent to let go of the need for control and to allow the child to sink or swim on his own merits. Usually, (although there are no guarantees) when an attached, angry, enmeshed child is allowed to "tough it out" on his own, or when the child experiences the outcomes of his way of doing things, he will turn things around. Many times, when a parent lets go of the need for control, the child will escalate negative behaviors to get the parent reinvolved in the negative cycle. But when the parent successfully resists the child's invitations to fight and argue, the child learns more acceptable ways to seek out the parent as a viable source of support and validation in daily living.

The failure to resolve an oppositional-defiant situation is the failure of the parent to allow for the child to be an individual. If the parent does not allow the child to separate, the child will continue to fight and is likely to find herself in either a passive-aggressive, hostile-dependent or an angry-alienated (i.e., emotionally divorced) relationship with that parent. All three can be viewed as the price for a parent's refusal to let go of the need to control.

A parent who struggles with enmeshment-oriented oppositionalism is usually a parent who has not learned that he can control only the environment in which the child lives, rather than the child himself (Principle 3). If oppositional systems are not successfully resolved early enough in a child's life, the negative results can last a lifetime. Two outcomes of failed individuation, hostile-dependency and angry-alienation will be examined in the following few paragraphs; the special case of the passive-aggressive classification follows later.

The *hostile-dependent* child represents a blended variation of the oppositional-defiant and the frightened-clingy styles. Notice in Figure 6 (page 101) that the location of this style is somewhat aggressive, yet closer to neutrality on the aggressive-timid axis and highly enmeshed on the enmeshed/estranged axis. This location reflects the notion that the hostile-dependent child is as fearful as he is aggressive. The child settles on hostile-dependency as a middle ground between her aggressive nature and the fear that she cannot meet life's demands without the assistance (enmeshment) of the ever-handy parents.

A parent in these situations will often insist that the young person do things for himself, only to step in at the last minute to save the child from the consequences of his actions (mistakes). Again, this rescue is a result of the parent's fear (i.e., unresolved separation anxiety) that the child cannot face life's problems independently, will fail, and will suffer irreparable damage if not rescued.

This rescue is an attempt on the parent's part to escape the extreme anxiety of feeling like a bad parent due to the fact that the youngster's failure is experienced as a personal failure by the parent. Eventually, the child will internalize the parent's fears, and will unconsciously believe, yet visibly act-out, her own lack of self-confidence. This dynamic is often manifest in the young person who acts and talks as though she can be independent and self-reliant, but proves to be a person of little substance and follow-through.

Often, hostile-dependency is revealed in older adolescents and young adults, but can be seen in younger children as well. Hostile-dependency is perpetuated by a grudge that exists between the parents and child, a grudge that does not disappear with generous gestures or beneficence on the part of the parents. Parents with hostile dependent children are usually parents who have failed to exercise Principles 1 (unconditional love) and 3 (limits of control). consider the following:

> Amanda Jackson hates her father; he is overbearing, self-centered, rude, and inconsiderate. Her mother hates him as well and left him four years ago. Her father is wealthy and uses his wealth as a way to control others. Yet for all her contempt, Amanda accepts all of her father's attempts to buy her love; she accepted the fifty dollar per week allowance at age thirteen, the fine clothes he bought for her throughout high school, the money for the mink stole for her senior prom, the car he purchased for her graduation (which she wrecked three weeks later), and she will accept his money to attend college in the fall.
>
> Amanda's dad is confused and angry because it seems that despite his efforts, that no matter what he does for her, Amanda doesn't appreciate him; she continues to treat him with disdain and contempt; naturally, he becomes ever more critical of and condescending toward Amanda.

Amanda and her father are linked in an embrace of enmeshment (i.e., emotional entanglement) brought on by dependence and anger; a dance that is likely to be transferred to Amanda's wealthy future husband, and later to their children.

The resolution to such a dilemma is best provided by the party who is the object of the dependency: the parent. This must be done by facing difficult feelings of guilt, powerlessness and anger, all the while pulling out of the habit of rescuing the offspring. There will be hard feelings, but in the long run the parent will likely experience the rewards of seeing the offspring fend for himself (and succeed). However, the longer a parent waits to remedy the hostile-dependent situation, the worse things will get; sometimes hostile-dependent relationships will last until the death of the parent doing the rescuing.

The *angry-alienated* relationship is another aspect of the failure to resolve the opposite-defiant situation. This situation is usually a result for children who are aggressive and self-determined enough to eventually totally pull away from the parent. In this case, the parent refuses to allow for adequate separation and continually badgers the child to comply with ongoing suggestions, recommendations, and/or direct commands and demands for compliance. Eventually the child comes to realize that the only way to achieve any sense of healthy separateness is to be completely divorced from that parent.

These children grow into young adults who would rather live in sheer squalor than to have to be dependent upon anyone, let alone their overbearing and demanding parents. Many times, these offspring will secretly maintain a relationship with the lesser controlling, more loving parent, and maintain hard feelings with the more tyrannical parent. Offspring from these relationships might find it easy to start romantic relationships with the opposite sex, but will have great difficulty maintaining them due to anger and control issues. As adults these offspring are often opinionated and self-righteous with a great deal of internalized anger fueling a great deal of irrational thought.

Hostile-dependent and angry-alienated relationships are perpetuated by a grudge that exists between the parent and child. This grudge has its origins in the anger that arises from the child's frustration regarding the parent's unconscious refusal to allow for separation in toddlerhood and is compounded by the parent's later demands that the child "should" be able to separate, but isn't capable (i.e., needs the parent's help), or doesn't do so according to the parent's expectations.

This grudge does not disappear with generous gestures, good intentions nor angry pronouncements on the part of the parent, nor does this grudge disappear with increased age (actually hostile-dependency and angry-alienation typically becomes stronger through young adulthood). Parents must realize that the only way to resolve these two situations is to let go of the need for control; there will be heartache on both sides to be sure, but the sooner the break, the sooner the child and the parent can experience a more harmonious, less entangled relationship. Short of this solution, the child will have to grow up, get into an intimate relationship (or remain painfully alone), fail in some way, and then seek professional assistance for unraveling the mystery of his difficult life. Many times this occurs after the death of the parents.

Successful resolution of the *angry-alienated* situations depends on the parent's ability to remove herself from the negative enmeshment that is experienced with the child. In this case (as well as hostile-dependency) the parent must be able to pull back and allow the child to experience his feelings without retribution or punishment, allowing the child to experience the consequences for making his own decisions; all in an attitude of love. It is of the utmost importance that a parent learns that it is she who must withdraw from the negative relationship rather than expect the child to do so. Children, even adult children, react and respond to parents; change in the parent-child diad occurs most readily when the parent leads the way.

Another common dynamic within enmeshed relationships results when a weary parent struggles to encourage separation, but does so through ineffective means. One common pattern adopted by the weary, ineffective parent is to attempt to instill guilt by way of playing the *martyr. Martyrdom* is a personality style adopted by many people who find themselves unable to be strong enough to effect executive decisions by any means other than guilting others into bending to their will.

Martyrs are parents who want their children to appreciate all the really good things they do for them. This parent uses guilt to manipulate the youngster toward compliance, guilt that is generated out of the parent's own aches, pains, and difficulties. Usually, whenever the child has a complaint or a criticism of this parent, the parent will upstage him with information regarding the parent's own difficult life, and very soon the child is overwhelmed by the parent's own complaints.

Often, this parent will bend over backwards to help others, including his own children, only to complain that no one ever helps in return. He is usually bitter and harbors the internal belief that others just don't care enough and are therefore inferior people.

The parent who plays the martyr is often secretly loathed by her child, yet the child will continually yield to the parent's requests out of a sense of duty which has been instilled since early childhood. Sometimes the child is not aware of the parent's martyrdom until early adulthood, and will at that time recoil and reject the parent's efforts to use this form of guilt.

Many children who, as adults, separate from their martyred parents will suffer a prolonged period of excommunication sustained by the parent's belief that the child is being ungrateful, insensitive and self-centered.

Resolution of martyrdom situations often requires professional assistance due to the risk of total alienation between the child and parent when the child (usually as an adult) finally stops yielding to the parent's attempts at compliance through guilt.

The Special Case of the Passive-aggressive Dynamic

A review of Figure 6 (page 101) reveals that the *passive-aggressive* style of interacting exists in all four quadrants. The reason for this is that the passive-aggressive style is largely a result of anger, fear, and a sense of powerlessness. Passive-aggressive techniques are usually employed in situations where the person feels that an open display of negative feeling will result in either dismissal or retribution. *Passive-aggressive* techniques can be employed by both estranged and enmeshed individuals who have learned that assertiveness results in punishment; however, the goals for the two differ.

The goal for the enmeshed passive-aggressive child is to communicate anger, fear and powerlessness to the parent without having to use actual words. Very often, the child will be unconsciously trying to get a message (e.g., "Don't bother me") to the parent, but is just too frightened to do so openly because the child fears losing the parent's love. Whereas, the estranged passive-aggressive child is adept at tricking and angering people just because she desires power; love is of no concern. The enmeshed child wants to communicate, the estranged child simply wants to have power.

Fig. 9

Passive-aggressive acting-out can be manifested in these classic ways: A child...

- seems never able to find a particular item when the parent sends her to fetch it
- continually takes parental belongings without permission, and without returning them
- steals
- lies when the truth would be far less painful
- deliberately fools around and drags her feet while doing some assigned task
- refuses to bathe but pretends to do so
- underachieves at school
- dresses weirdly in defiance of the parent
- fails in an important situation (e.g., the big game, SATs, auditions, first impressions, etc.)

These examples are have several things in common:

- they represent situations that are more important to the parent than to the youngster
- the youngster is likely irritated or angry that she is being *told* to do something undesirable at a time that is inconvenient (i.e., most of the time)
- the child does not feel safe stating negative feelings to the parent
- every situation as mentioned above will yield an angry parent (i.e., the payoff for the passive-aggressive style of interacting)

By acting helpless or hapless the child can successfully transfer his own feelings of fear, anger and powerlessness to the parent. When the parent becomes angry and punitive, the child then takes on the role of the victim, often able to play on the sympathies of certain others (e.g., teachers, neighbors, and relatives).

The *passive-aggressive* style of interacting is especially infuriating for a parent because it is extremely difficult to prove that the child is deliberately or subconsciously trying to anger the parent. Often, when the parent confronts the situation with the child, the child will play stupid or innocent, making the parent seem paranoid. Enmeshed or estranged, the *passive-aggressive* personality style is an extremely effective, albeit self-defeating, tool for a young person to transfer negative feelings to adults.

Resolution of the *passive-aggressive* situation requires a great deal of patience on the part of the adults in the system. The enmeshed (attached) child will have to learn to talk about feelings with her parent and the parent will have to learn how to tolerate verbal negativity from the child. The estranged (unattached) passive-aggressive child will require a multi-year regimen of expert, professional intervention to achieve some sort of connection with an adult and to possibly gain a desire to seek approval rather than power.

The Avoidant-estranged Child:
Adoptive and foster Children (Quadrant III)

The avoidant-estranged child is one who is born with an avoidant temperament and has experienced a lack of attachment in infancy or a broken attachment at some point early in her life. There are three levels of functioning that are identified for these children.

As noted above, the first style of relating in this quadrant is *passive-aggressive;* the next is revealed in the *passive-resistant* child. Passive-resistant children seem very similar to passive-aggressive children, but differ in goals rather than behavior. Whereas the passive-aggressive child wants to anger the parent, the passive-resistant child simply wants to avoid doing something that she deems unpleasant; an angry parent is a result but not the primary objective. The passive-resistant child is the estranged compliment to the enmeshed frightened-clingy child in that a pattern of negative enmeshment (i.e., power struggles) is set up when adults insist that the passive-resistant child perform at a level higher than she desires.

A *passive-resistant* child has usually internalized a great deal of shame and self-doubt and avoids these feelings by making vain attempts

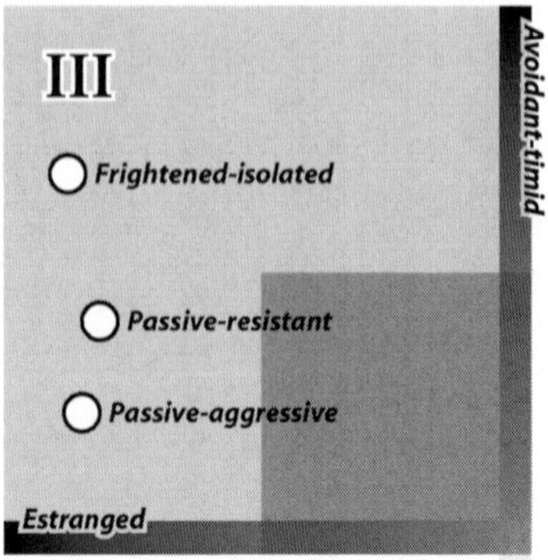

Fig. 10

to succeed or not even trying at all. This child sets out to fail and thereby achieves success by being a failure.

Resolution of this situation is a time consuming process that requires a great deal of patience. This child must be shown that he can experience success along the lines of what is socially and societally acceptable. Success of this nature must start small and eventually build into significant achievements. These successes are often hard fought because the closer the child gets to experiencing a true success, the greater will be his anxiety regarding failure. This increased anxiety can be so pronounced that the child often reverts to the passive-resistant mode because it is familiar.

The final avoidant-estranged style of relating is the *frightened-isolated* situation. This style of interacting is best represented by a child who wants to avoid contact with the outside world. He tends to be a loner with few or no friends; he attends school, but sits in the back of the room and does just enough work to avoid recognition.

This child's difficulties are likely to be discovered in the school setting because she is found out to be an underachiever. The adults in the system begin to pressure the child to perform at a higher level. When this happens the child usually recoils and will withdraw or even runaway and hide. This child is not necessarily angry or hostile, but is terrified of life's demands and will make every effort to find a way to avoid them.

The resolution of the *frightened-isolated* style of interacting requires a great deal of patience and time. These children need adults who are interested in them, but are not pushy to the point that the child's inner terror is activated. The major goal for relating with this type of child is to simply connect with the child. Adults who attempt to relate to this child must take on the persona of an animal trainer who must at first gain enough trust for the animal to accept food, let alone some form of formal training. Professional assistance is required, to both reach the child and to help the adults in the child's world cope with the difficult feelings that emerge when working through these difficult situations.

The Aggressive-estranged Situation: Adopted and Foster Children (Quadrant IV)

This quadrant describes the most serious of all the interactional systems. It is here, in the aggressive-estranged system, that anger and hatred can exist with little or no internal limitation on the part of the child, for there is no guilt, no conscience.

The *oppositional-defiant* estranged child (i.e., unattached) has a very different operational agenda than does the oppositional-defiant enmeshed

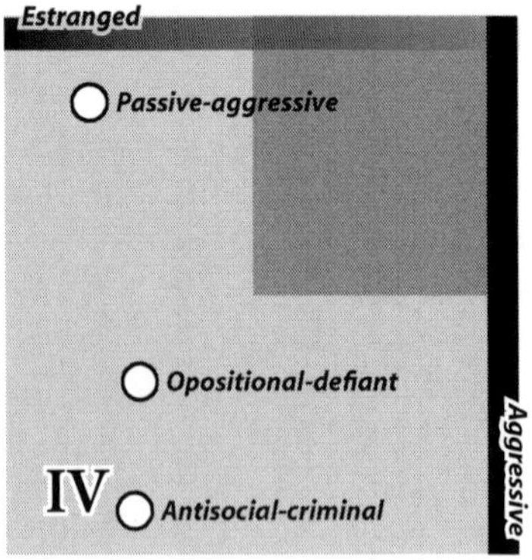

Fig. 11 *Aggressive-estranged (Quadrant IV)*

child. Whereas the enmeshed child is resisting the enmeshment and is unconsciously working to gain freedom, the estranged child is craving enmeshment and welcomes it as a source of power and connection. The aggressive-estranged child pulls others close to him by angering or terrorizing them and thereby acquiring constant attention.

This constant attention, albeit negative and unappealing to adult caretakers and authority figures, is reminiscent of the constant attention that should have been received in infancy. This child is not interested in acquiring freedom, he wants control; he does not want approval, he wants power. He will not grow out of his need for power, nor develop a sense of connectedness to the society as a whole; his anger and hatred will be reinforced by the punitive responses received at the hands of adults and authorities. This child is unconscionable and completely self-serving.

The fact that these children set up negative encounters with others in their world insures that they will internalize huge amounts of anger and toxic shame (see *Shame: a Brief Dissertation,* page 135) as a result of the anger being pumped into them by adults and others. This is a very hard process to stop because it is a result of behaviors from the child that seem to clearly merit anger on the part of adults. The child's inner world becomes more and more affected with rage and shame, and thus, the child will show less and less concern for others (i.e., no conscience).

The resolution for the estranged oppositional-defiant system is not as easy as the resolution for the enmeshed child. When the enmeshed child is left to flounder, she is most likely to learn her lesson and grow up. When the estranged child is left to flounder, he will create enough trouble in the environment to eventually obtain the constant attention and external care required to resume a safe balance of hatred and control. Left untreated, the oppositional-defiant estranged child is likely to develop into a full-blown *antisocial* personality: a person who is totally devoid of any feeling or concern for any other than himself; a person incapable of experiencing conscience.

The *antisocial* person is highly likely to enter the criminal justice system and find himself in jail, a place that will provide all the care and structure that he needs to remain non-threatening to society.

Interventions for resolving this very difficult personality style need to be applied at a very young age. This means that certain adults (e.g., teachers, doctors, ministers, and such) need to be able to recognize these children early in life and provide help for them as quickly as possible. Success depends on a very special arrangement for the child in her environment. In order for the aggressive-estranged child to recover from the internal damage already done, a structured yet loving environment is required. A world that is constructed as a boot camp, but with compassionate drill sergeants, is one way to meaningfully intervene before these children are too old to be reached.

As noted earlier, the styles of relating in estranged situations are often seen in adoptive and foster care situations. Many adoptive and foster children come from less than optimum prenatal and neonatal situations. Very often, the fact that an unwanted child has been separated from her birth mother automatically severs an already damaged parent-child bond, and thus the child-parent bond is not likely to form without extremely hard work on the part of other adults in the child's world. These children are difficult throughout their childhoods in that their relational goals are opposite those of the attached or enmeshed children: they are much more concerned with power and control rather than separation, love and approval.

Many caring and well-intentioned adults want to step up and help the estranged and aggressive child, but they must be very careful about doing so. These adults must be aware of the many pitfalls that will be encountered with the aggressive-estranged child, especially when the adults attempt to deal with this child as if the child were seeking attachment. It must be remembered that the goal of these types of children is nearly always the same, i.e., to defeat the adult.

The Ideal Relationship

Now that the reader has examined the various styles of parent-child relationships, it is likely that a question has begun to present itself: "So what does an ideal parent-child relationship look like?"

First, a few assumptions will be laid out to set the stage for the ideal relationship:

- the parent has read, understands, and practices the *Principles of Powerful Parenting* (see page xvi)
- child and parent are bonded in a love relationship from infancy
- the parent understands that there is no more important job than parenting
- any of the four styles of relating can occur in an average family (particularly in adolescence), and can be handled relatively well as long as not in the extreme.

So what then is ideal?

An ideal relationship is one in which both parties are satisfied with its overall quality. The ideal relationship is somewhat like a game of pitch and catch. As long as things are going well and the ball is tossed and caught with ease, there will be few problems. But if the game gets harder, or if the players tire, the ball will be missed, and the quality of the experience can change quickly.

There are several things that can happen when the ball is missed:

- the one who missed it can blame the one who threw it
- the one who threw it can blame the one who missed it
- the one who missed it can claim fault and the one who threw it can say that yes, indeed it was (or vice versa)

But ideally, the person who missed it can say that the miss was his fault and the person who threw it can say that he could have thrown it better. When this happens, the true cooperative spirit of the game comes through and both demonstrate that each somehow realizes that the game involves two people and that no matter what happens, both are responsible.

Ideal family relationships appear somewhat like this: Parents must learn they are not always right, and realize the child is not always wrong or at fault. Family relationships are forced relationships for the children; that is, they didn't sign up for the experience; it just happens that they are there. It helps when parents are friendly (but not necessarily friends) with the child.

Parents have to learn to listen more than they talk, allow more than they prohibit, act more than lecture, trust more than they mistrust, and always be true to their word. A good parent does not deny a child's reality by denying the child his feelings; a good parent teaches that honesty is preferable to perfection, and is willing to admit error and provide apologies when necessary.

A responsible parent realizes that loving a child and indulging a child are two completely different things; no parent is doing his child a favor by giving her everything she wants, when she wants it. Parents help their children immeasurably when they insist that they earn much of what they get. Further, it greatly helps children learn to cope better when parents learn to express genuine empathy for the pain that accompanies life's difficulties and hard knocks (rather than shaming them with ridicule or criticism).

The responsible parent learns that she must teach a child that material things (especially those of others) are important, but that relationships are more so; that love is a verb that overrides the desire to hurt others. The good parent models compassion with a firm sense of self and personal identity.

A responsible parent learns to find ways to motivate a child to do things that may be undesirable (e.g., a chore or punishment), yet help the child to achieve pride in his efforts. A good parent seeks ways to help her child "save face" in embarrassing or shame-producing situations that involve the parent. In the end, the ideal parent-child relationship is one in which both the child and the parent like each other and continue to do so throughout their lives. The ideal relationship is different for different people, but the defining element of the ideal relationship is that it is mutually satisfactory to both parent and child. If this isn't happening, then reread this book.

If that doesn't do it, talk to a minister, a counselor, a friend, or anybody else who is willing to talk straight to you so that you can learn about yourself what your child already knows.

Worksheet

1. Consider one of your children and refer to Figure 1 (page 90):

   • how old is the child you're thinking about?______

   • do you consider your child to be an average, ordinary child (i.e., non-handicapped; do not include ADHD or ADD as a handicap)?______

   • considering the material presented regarding mothering, parenting, and relating, what percentage will you rate yourself with this child in each category?

   ______% Mothering

   ______% Parenting

   ______% Relating
   (100% total)

2. Consider the same child as above, then explain the principles of mothering, relating and parenting to someone who is close to you; get her opinion as to how she would rate you in each category.

3. Did you see yourself in the same way as the other person sees you? Close? Where is the biggest difference? What are your thoughts about any differences that may be present?

4. Do you think parents should have a voice in how their teens dress? Why or why not?

5. Once again, consider the same child as above. Is she aggressive or avoidant (think easy vs. hard)?

   ____

   Has your child learned to be assertive?________

   Place your child on the continuum:

6. Do you see yourself as aggressive, assertive, or avoidant? Ask your spouse or someone close to you to classify you; examine any difference in the perceptions. If there are differences, how do you explain them?

7. Have you ever been told that you are either hot or cold, on or off, black or white? If so, has being this way created problems for you? How?

8. Now that you have read about splitting, who in your world has the tendency to see the world in extremes rather than blends? What has it been like for you to relate with this person?

9. Revisit the story of Dominic and Milo; identify two other triangles in that example. Can you offer an explanation as to why the family has such a hard time getting along?

What do the parents need to learn to do?

10. Revisit the relationship continuum (figure 3, page 96) and reconsider your subject person; where do the two of you fit on that continuum? Check your view with someone close to the both of you. Resolve any difference. Locate your relationship with your subject child on the following continuum.

11. Using the locations you have already plotted in questions 5 and 10, use the graph on page 90 to plot the location of your relationship with your subject child.

12. Refer to Figure 4 (page 98). How does your estimation of your relationship with your subject child fit with the styles represented there? Are you pleased, surprised, or disappointed with your result? Why?

13. Consider each of the following parent-child relationships (name someone with whom you are familiar for each of the categories):

    - frightened-clingy
    - oppositional defiant
    - martyrdom
    - hostile dependent
    - angry-alienated

14. Now that you have examined the relationship you have with one of your children, how do you feel about the results? What might you need to do to make the relationship better? Can you visualize yourself in an ideal relationship with this child after the child grows to maturity?

APPENDIX

INTERVENTIONS

The interventions that follow are the result of more than twenty years of practice as a therapist, counselor, and parent educator. They were not taken from any book or source that can be identified for any one intervention, but rather are recommendations and encouragements that have been found to work for parents when dealing with their children.

These behavioral recommendations are arranged in developmental order and presented in a way that logically flows from one into another.

For the most part, each intervention is self-contained and can be used by parents without professional supervision; however, as with any attempt to alter the course of human behavior, professional assistance is recommended.

It is very difficult to change things for others when the self is ignored in the process.

As noted in the Foreword, what follows is truly representative of what one man has learned from his mistakes.

INFANCY: MIDDLE OF THE NIGHT

Every parent knows that many times during the life of an infant, he will awaken in the night and require some sort of assistance. Naturally, it is the parent's job to resolve the problem. There will be many times, however, when the parent finds nothing is needed; the child just wants to be held (which in itself is a need).

If this happens frequently enough, weary parents are likely to get frustrated and irritated; negative emotions will generally make the situation worse.

Many parents are taught the old adage "let him cry himself to sleep" by well-meaning grandparents, and think that to tend to a crying child is "spoiling" that child. Nothing could be further from the truth, and during nighttime, nothing is worse for most children (i.e., noncolickly).

When a non-colicky infant cries in the night for no apparent reason, it is likely that the child wants contact with the parent; it is important to remember that touch and physical contact are basic human needs. Therefore, if the parent does not go to the child, the child suffers an unmet need and the trust between the child and the parent may be compromised.

A good strategy for handling these types of situations is as follows:

When a parent is awakened by a crying child, she should immediately start talking to the child from the parent's room with soft reassuring sounds, tones and words. These words should convey a sense of safety to the child. As the parent puts on slippers and bathrobe, and walks to the child's room, the reassuring talk should continue. Soft talk, the sound of mother's bathrobe being put on, the walk to the child's room, and the eventual contact with the child all set up a series of familiar events inside the child's mind.

Once the parent gets to the child's room, the child should be examined for dirty diapers, pain, fever, hunger or other physical sources of discomfort. If nothing is found to be the matter, the parent should console the child with soft words and acceptance. After a time, the mother can return the child to the crib and allow for the child to return to sleep. Mother or father can then return to the bedroom. Please note: allowing the child to fall asleep in the crib rather than in the parent's arms will increase the tendency for the child to fall asleep with the parent near, but without having to be held by the parent.

When this procedure is performed repeatedly, the child will learn that the sound of the parent's voice will be followed by the arrival of that loving parent. The child will associate mother's (or father's) voice with the relief that he has time and again experienced, and is likely to fall back asleep before the parent gets to the crib unless, of course, there is something more pressing for the child than just needing reassurance and touch.

Please Note

This intervention is not suited for colicky babies. Colicky children should be managed with the utmost concern and will often require the assistance of a pediatrician.

COLIC: AN ATTACHMENT PERSPECTIVE

Colic is a condition that affects about 20% of all infant children; it usually starts at about two or three weeks of age and lasts two or three months (some cases can last up to six months). There are various explanations as to why a child develops colic, but regardless of the reason, it can be concluded that the colicky child is in continuous distress.

Trust and Love

As noted in the first part of this book, love and trust are two of the most important ingredients for the development of a healthy person; trust is a result of the process of the continual successful gratification of an infant's needs.

The trust cycle unfolds as follows:

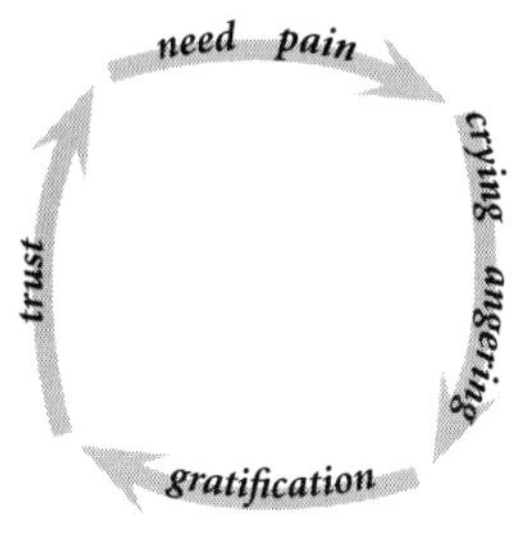

When this cycle is repeated on a continual and consistent basis the child will internalize a healthy amount of trust that will last for the rest of his life. When this does not happen, the child's ability to internalize trust will be compromised and it is likely that a larger than desired amount of mistrust will result, and the quality of the child-mother bond will be less than optimal. Increased mistrust and diminished bonding will often give way to difficult and undesirable behaviors in the child's development (e.g., lying, stealing, deceitfulness, anger, and depression) which can result in serious relationship difficulties in adulthood.

As for love, it is the mother eyes and face that provide the mirror in which the child first sees herself, and when she sees love in that mirror, love for the mother grows within the child. If this mirror is clouded by the effects of mother's unsuccessful efforts to provide rest and relief to her baby, then failure and futility will be absorbed into the core of the child's being. In order for the child to develop as healthily as possible, this "mirror" must be clear and must reflect mother's love in order for the child to absorb that love in the first few months of life.

Recommendations

The parent of a colicky child should consult the child's pediatrician regarding the physical sources for the child's discomfort. If the doctor is unable to find a root physical cause, then the parent and the doctor must work together to find ways to relieve the child's pain.

Non-medical

First, a parent should seek a non-medical method for providing relief and comfort. Many parents have found that placing the child in a car seat on top of a running dryer will soothe the child to sleep; other parents have found that automatic swings with music will work; still others find that taking their child for a drive around the block a few times will do the trick. A parent must consult friends and family for various methods that have proved successful for other children, and then try them all.

It is of the utmost importance that the parent does not take the position of "let him cry himself to sleep" in that the child will only grow more frustrated and alienated from the love of the parent. Lastly, there are a large number of websites on the internet that offer various solutions for colic; care should be taken to avoid "snake oil" remedies that are touted as curative; many of these "cures" are simply attempts to prey on people's desperation.

Medical: an Opinion

There are cases, however, when parents are unable to find anything that will bring relief to the child, and the child will get to sleep due only to exhaustion; this sleep is usually brief and the child resumes crying in a very short time. These situations should be brought to the attention of a doctor and the parent can petition the doctor to provide a pain reliever or medical intervention that will alleviate the colic symptoms.

Usually, doctors are resistant to provide medical remedies to these situations because the drugs used are Class 2 narcotics such as codeine or opiate derivatives, and the doctor does not want to create an addiction for the child.

Thus, in the grand scheme of things in a child's life, a choice must be made for the child: pain with no medicine, or relief with addiction. The choice to refrain from certain viable medical interventions could result in months of ongoing pain with little or no relief provided by the mother (or primary caretaker). This choice disrupts the trust cycle and the child will not learn to associate relief with mother's presence. In addition, the mother's countenance becomes negative and the child not only experiences physical pain, but the added pain of rejection which is absorbed from the weary mother's efforts to cope with a chronically stressful situation.

On the other hand, if the parent and the doctor agree to use a narcotic or some other medical pain reliever to ease the child's pain, the child will learn to associate relief with mother's presence and the trust cycle will be resumed. After about three months, the symptoms of colic will usually begin to disappear, and the mother and the doctor can begin a program to wean the child from the medicine. Within a year the colic will be gone, any drug dependency will be severed, and the damage done by the colic will be minimized.

There are numerous websites available on the internet that will explain colic and offer various remedies; *http://www.americanbaby.com* was used for some of the information supplied in this section.

Conclusion

Where food and water provide the basics for human subsistence, trust and love provide the basics for healthy personality development. The circumstances brought about by colic compromise both trust and love. Above all, these two elements of human development must be maintained throughout infancy; whatever means are necessary to relieve a crying infant should be employed as often as necessary throughout the first year of a child's life. This will insure that trust will grow within the child and that love will unfold within the mother-child bond.

PSYCHOLOGICAL JUDO: AN OVERVIEW

Americans live in a society of individualism and oppositionalism. Sadly, our first response to most things that bother us is to fight them, and what seems to have happened in recent years is that adversarialism and competition have become the rule. Cooperation has become less and less the optimum way to do things.

Psychological judo is born of the notion that it is better to go along with another's resistance than to go against it. In the world of martial arts, there are a variety of schools of defense that use the other's momentum to render him ineffective in an attack. These methods of disarming an adversary are also non-retaliatory and tend to invite less aggression from the "opponent" over the long-term. What follows are the basic elements of psychological judo.

Be Careful What —ou Wish for, for Surely —ou Will Get It

Some time ago, a wife and husband were attending night classes through their school district to learn the fundamentals of investing. The instructor told a story of a very wealthy man who was being questioned by a journalist preparing a feature about him. One of the questions concerned how he managed to get so wealthy in the stock market. His reply was simple... "when people wanted to sell, I bought; when they wanted to buy, I sold." This attitude about affording others what they want is the central element to using psychological judo.

Inertia

We all have had experiences with small children who want to play with us. Often in that play, we adults will take one of the child's hands, and the child will attempt to pull away. If we simply let go of the child, the child's backward momentum will carry him or her to the ground, often with a thump, and often followed by tears. This phenomenon is a very simple, yet very clear, example of how the other person's inertia (i.e., momentum) works to undo the "other."

Parenting and Psychological Judo

Understanding and using psychological judo in parent-child relationships can make the difference between a healthy, well-adjusted youngster and an overly dependent or totally oppositional child. The wise parent knows to let the child's inertia take him to where he is going to go; the parent then remains available to help the child reassemble the pieces "after the fall."

Consider:

> An eight year-old little girl gets a new pair of shoes that she desperately wants to show off at school on Monday because everybody in the class has been talking about these shoes, but no one has a pair yet. It snows Sunday evening, and by Monday morning the streets and sidewalks are covered with snow, ice, and slush.
>
> The parent warns that it would not be a good idea for her to wear the new shoes in the snow and ice because the salt that has been used on the streets and sidewalks will damage the new (and expensive) shoes. She begins to cry, saying that they are her shoes and that she wants to wear them, and that her old shoes don't fit, and that nobody wears overshoes to school because only "geeks" wear them.
>
> Many parents would simply say *No,* and risk a power struggle, but psychological judo could be applied here to provide a learning experience instead of an argument.
>
> Think of what might happen if the parent simply and knowingly said, "Yes, but you know it's very messy out there this morning, maybe you should wait until tomorrow to wear them," and then simply allowed the child to wear the new shoes.
>
> Initially, the child would be ecstatic that she gets to wear the shoes. Then she puts them on and heads out the door into the snow. She goes to the bus stop and waits without making another move until the bus comes; she gets on the bus and sits in her seat. At the next stop Jeffrey Izenstinkle gets on the bus with his size eleventy-seven galoshes and heads for his seat in the back of the bus. As he passes your daughter he tramples her new shoes, and she immediately goes into a quiet rage; shortly thereafter she hears your voice inside head saying "it's pretty messy out there; maybe you should wait until tomorrow to wear them." She silently seethes, and vows to pummel "Jeffrey the geek" with snow balls at recess. Before recess comes, however, she goes to the restroom, cleans her shoes as

> best she can and gets her name on the board for taking too much time out of the class; now she's going to "kill" Jeffrey as soon as no one is looking.
>
> Next the teacher announces that, yes, recess will be outside, but the children need to be aware that the snow has yet to be scraped from the playground. Your daughter beams until she realizes that the only way to exact her revenge on Jeffrey will be to go outside and slog through the snow, thus making a greater mess of her new shoes. She wisely decides to stay in for recess to keep her shoes dry and neat; all the while trying to figure a way to keep that idiot Jeffrey off her feet while on the bus ride home. It is at this point that she makes a promise to herself to never wear her good shoes in bad weather again unless the "geek ban" on overshoes is lifted.

This example illustrates how important it is for the parent to trust that a child can, and will, value herself and her things enough to make choices which can lead to valuable lessons. Psychological judo, as the underpinning for a parent's philosophy, will help the parent and the child move in a more healthy direction. Sometimes, giving children what they want and letting them learn from their mistakes can be more beneficial and palatable than taking on the role of "benevolent" dictator and making all of a child's life decisions.

This next example contrasts differences between "traditional parenting" and psychological judo when a youth displays thoughts and feelings that might sometimes be considered inappropriate or unacceptable:

> You are the parent of a fifteen year old boy who lets it be known that he is angry at you because he is "grounded" to the home for a week because he had company in the house while you were away from the home. Your son maintains that you are being "unfair" because you did not remind him to have no visitors immediately before you left the house (although, the "no visitors" rule has been in effect since kindergarten).
>
> You know that part of your son's anger is because he wants to go to a concert production on Friday evening. You remind him that he wouldn't have this problem if he had only done the right thing in the first place. Further, you emphasize your point by lecturing him about the evils of his "rotten" music to the point that he becomes

> furious with you and calls you a "jerk." This requires further punishment for showing disrespect. In the end he is punished more severely and is grounded for even a longer period of time for being so disrespectful.
>
> But if the principles of psychological judo were employed, you would allow him to be angry at you, and in fact, could welcome his anger with some empathy (e.g., "I don't blame you for being mad at me, I know that it hurts to be punished"). You would maintain your stance in the matter of his restriction, but show some concern for how he is affected by the situation. You would refrain from any derogatory comments about his world and his "type," and you would disconnect from his attempts to bait you with his negativity.
>
> He then has far less incentive to continue his ranting exchange. You maintained your insistence on the consequence, but you showed some understanding for his position; in the end he is stuck with having to face the inevitable. He has been "allowed" his feelings, but he learns that his feelings won't change things.

Of course, there is no guarantee that this latter approach would defuse the situation, but it is clear that it does much to keep things from getting worse (and often times, not making things worse is the best that one can do in an unpleasant exchange). This is an example of psychological judo in personal communication.

Conclusion

Overall, learning to negotiate the difficulties in life by finding ways to go along, helps to reduce fighting and thus increase personal peace and "okayness." Learning to "go along to get along" is not necessarily a forfeiture of one's pride or integrity; quite to the contrary, learning to allow others to live with their own problems is much better than becoming a problem for them (or visa versa).

How does one employ psychological judo on a daily basis? Actually it is quite simple. When a child wants permission to do a thing that you feel is "wrong," but is not dangerous, then sometimes it is okay to say "Yes"; this allows you to step back and watch the child learn a lesson. If this process can be executed confidently with empathy, and without fear, anxiety, or the hidden anger of disapproval, it will yield an additional stone in the foundation of the child's developing character.

MOTIVATION, CONSEQUENCE AND PUNISHMENT: UNDERSTANDING PARENTAL INTENTIONS

Although what follows is not a specific intervention, it will outline the very important differences between effective and ineffective approaches to handling discipline issues with children.

In order for parents to be more successful in their efforts to raise responsible children, they will need to distinguish between the need for either motivation, consequence, or punishment. Doing so will yield a much greater degree of harmony and cooperation.

To begin, a parent must understand that there are two realms of behavior to be addressed: the desirable and undesirable. Further, a parent must realize that there are three variables that affect desirable and undesirable behaviors: whether the behavior in question is occurring in the present, has occurred in the past, and could occur in the future.

There is a very different approach for handling past desirable behaviors as opposed to those that were undesirable; likewise, there is a very significant difference between dealing with future behaviors that are either desirable or otherwise.

It is crucial that a parent learns to think in the above terms when dealing with behaviors in a child because the parent must know his goal and whether or not that goal can be achieved with the method at hand.

The Essence of Punishment

Punishment is a process that has been used by parents since the human species began. Parents use punishment as a response to an undesirable behavior that has already occurred, or as a response to defiance and noncompliance. Punishments are usually doled out under the guise of teaching the child a lesson. Punishments usually inflict pain in the recipient, and are usually motivated by anger (they also result in increased anger and resentment from the one being punished).

Punishments are usually manifest by the following five categories:

- *Actual physical punishment.* Hitting, slapping, switching, whipping.
- *Threatening.* Implying some form of future retribution for failure to comply in the moment.
- *Guilting/shaming/belittling.* Saying things such as, "You really look stupid when you cry," or "You should know better than to do something like that."

- *Depriving.* Complete and total removal of some pleasant activity or enjoyable item. ("Since you didn't clean your room, you can't go to the dance on Friday.")
- *–elling and its opposite, shunning.*

Punishment and Effectiveness

Very often, punishments are used as a way to respond to some serious rule infraction or major life mistake (e.g., starting a fire or vandalizing a home) or for the parents to vent their own anger on their child(ren); however, punishments are not usually effective for gaining cooperation or compliance.

For the most part, punishment often becomes a relatively ineffective parenting tool, especially in families where it is over-used and has failed to bring about the desired results.

> ***Punishment needs to be reserved for situations in ..hich there is no apparent natural consequence for a given behavior that has already occurred. It should rarely, if ever, be used in situations in ..hich the parent is trying to motivate a youngster to do or accomplish something.***

Punishment is wholly ineffective as a motivational tool; its value lies in its usefulness as a deterrent to committing a specific act. Punishment should be used sparingly.

Punishment becomes ineffective when an angered parent employs it to inflict pain (under the guise of a deterrent) rather than use consequences to to allow the youngster to learn from her mistakes.

About Consequence

The notion of consequence (natural or logical) is quite different from that of punishment. Natural consequences are what occur when an act is committed in nature. For example, if a teenager speeds around a corner, loses control of the car, and has an accident, she experiences a natural consequence for driving too fast. When the teen's parents take away the privilege to drive for one month as a result of the fact that alcohol was involved, a logical consequence (in the form of a punishment) has been inflicted. both deter speeding in the future, but they differ by way of their origin and intent.

In nature there is nothing personal about a consequence; it happens irrespective of who is involved. Logical consequences are different, they resemble punishments, but are in some way logically connected the original infraction; typically, punishments are often unrelated to the committed act and are used to suit the "punisher's" desires rather than the child's needs.

Motivation and Compliance

Whenever a parent asks a youngster to perform some task (be it a chore, good grades, good manners, and etc.) the parent should be operating from a motivational stance. If the parent is trying to get the youngster to comply with a request, he should realize that the desired behavior is a future behavior (it has yet to occur), and that energy (work) is required on the part of the child. Punishments at this juncture are totally ineffective, especially in the long-run, because punishments will not motivate a person to work. After all, this is America in the 21st Century; people don't like to feel pushed around or be treated like imbeciles.

Whenever a parent is trying to motivate a child to do something, Win/Win techniques (see page 156) can be applied effectively. The parent becomes motivational when she keeps the focus on what is happening presently, or on what will happen shortly in the future. The parent is also being motivational when the child can see a favorable outcome for himself.

One of the biggest factors in motivating a child toward compliance is the child's ability to chose between outcomes. The process of Win/Win may not always yield what the parent wants, but it **always** results an adherence to the terms the parent has set forth (thus, compliance is achieved). In other words, parents find themselves upholding terms of their contracts with their children, and in so doing, will build trust (See *Win/Win Parenting, page* 156).

Motivation and Punishment

Ironically, punishment (i.e., a logical consequence) is itself a task which the parents must get the child to complete; thus, a punishment is something that needs to be motivated.

Once again, Win/Win Parenting techniques can be exercised. For example, Sally has spoken very rudely to her mother and mother has assigned the evening dishes to Sally as a punishment for her behavior; Sally resists and refuses. When mother tells her that she is grounded (another punishment) until she decides to wash, dry and put away the dishes, mother is actually providing a motivating factor (Sally's freedom); Sally will be motivated to get free of her restriction and will eventually agree to do the dishes. Mother will have to be patient and be certain to enforce the restriction, but the outcomes (i.e., choice and trust) are worth it.

Guideline Grid for Promoting Acceptable Behaviors

What follows is a matrix grid of the combinations of behaviors and time frames. It represents a way to envision parental perspectives in daily life with a child.

	Past	**Present**	**Future**
Desirable	Enouragement Rewards Praise	Encouragement Praise Joining in	Win/Win
Undesirable	Consequences Punishments	Blocking Stopping	Education

Desirable Behaviors

Past — When desirable behaviors have been exhibited, parents should take the time to show appreciation. Praise should be given for a job well done. Parents must be careful to refrain from overdoing praise in that the child is likely to feel that she is being manipulated (this is especially true for teens). *Remember to avoid criticism;* few things hurt as much as being told "you did a good job, but you should have..."

Present — While desirable behaviors are occurring, a parent can give praise and show appreciation for the effort. A parent can offer help to complete a given task and encourage cooperation. *Avoid criticism and attempts to take control.*

Future — Completion of future desirable behaviors (e.g., tasks, assignments, chores and etc.) requires motivation; Win/Win Parenting techniques provide a framework for successful parenting. *Avoid bribery and threats.*

Undesirable Behaviors

Past

When undesirable behaviors have already occurred, parents should take time to think about a reasonable consequence or punishment. Consider:

- Time-out
- Go To Your Room
- Grounding
- Restrictions of freedoms
- Work as punishment

Avoid angry responses. Always set a time limit on any restriction (except those imposed until compliance is achieved). Remember, defiance and noncompliance require motivational techniques, not punishment.

Present

Undesirable behaviors (arguing, fighting, destroying property, hurting self or others) that are occurring in the present require that the parent intervene to stop the behavior; parents must remember that arguments do not occur when the parent won't argue. *Avoid physical intimidation or use of unnecessary force.*

There is no one way to stop a behavior when it is occurring. Often parents will try to stop a child's behavior by telling the child to stop, only to find themselves in an argument. It has been found that when parents simply and persistently repeat the command to stop without getting side-tracked, the child will comply.

Blocking (restraining) a child's undesirable behaviors is best done with small children; sometimes there is no way to stop older children from doing what they are doing. In these cases it is necessary to wait for the situation to pass and then deal with the behavior as a past behavior.

Future

It is impossible for a parent to prevent a child from doing anything. The best way to improve possible future outcomes is to:

- Provide education about potential hazards
- Apply firm and reasonable execution of consequences and punishments when necessary
- Avoid lecturing
- Avoid worrying and feeling guilty

- Trust the child to make "right" choices. This single shift in a parent's thinking can result in increased conscionable behavior.

Use of this material in combination with the concept of motivation and Win/Win Parenting techniques can and will yield a much smoother disciplinary life for children and their parents. It is important for the individual parent to be able to see his location on the grid in any given instance and employ actions that will best address the parent's concerns and the child's needs.

Conclusion

For many generations, human beings have been reared by the use of punishment as the major way to produce socially acceptable behaviors. In the past (less than 3 generations ago) most people were poor with minimal resources and means. Punishments worked because people (children, as well) did not know any different, and punishments were socially accepted.

Today, our society is virtually filled with abundance. Even the lowest standards of living in the United States far outweigh the average living conditions in the past. Almost every person in the United States has access to a television and thus a model for how life is supposed to be. The 1960s brought about a shift in the country's views on civil (and Children's) rights; children today are protected from the very harsh treatments of the past, and are therefore granted a certain power to refuse (or report) severe treatment. Punishment, especially physical punishment, is basically banned throughout the society, and parents who were raised with punishments are at a loss for other ways to raise their children.

Punishment is a human concept, and a human application used to control and socialize our offspring. The use of punishment as a primary parenting tool is outmoded; newer, more effective methods of socialization are available.

It is time to use them.

SHAME: A BRIEF DISSERTATION

Shame: the undiscovered territory of being human.

A man can stand a lot, as
long as he can stand himself.
Axel Munthe

Shame is the hidden feeling which lies beneath most strong emotional responses to life's challenges, and it is the fear of experiencing shame that seems to be the basis of psychological defense mechanisms (e.g., denial, blame, rationalization, etc.) but, references to shame are scarcely present in psychology textbooks. It is interesting to note that treatment models have been developed for depression, anxiety, rage, and behavioral problems, yet there is virtually no mention of a "shame disorder" anywhere in the formal diagnostic manuals used by mental health professionals. If *affect theory* (see below) and the resulting shame theory are indeed valid and true, then our psychiatric and psychological communities are missing the mark in their ability to explain and treat various human conditions.

Affect Theory

Simply put, affect theory is a concept that views the human being as motivated by feelings (as opposed to unconscious drives or instincts). Examples of these feelings are fear, sorrow, excitement, anger, and shame. In all, there are nine feelings noted in the theory, but those noted above will serve the purposes of this discussion.

To adequately understand the feeling of shame as part of affect theory, we first look toward another, less misunderstood feeling: fear. Most people agree that fear is an appropriate response to a variety of experiences in daily life. Also, most agree that fear is not a learned response, but that it occurs naturally and is vital for survival. In other words, fear is not taught and learned; it is experienced and used. Naturally, different people perceive different things to be threatening, but overall, the feeling of fear is a universally understood experience. So it is with shame. The feeling of shame is a universally experienced response to personal failure in the human being. No other animal presents this response except humans (it is suspected that dogs can experience shame as a response to interactions with humans, but not independently within the canine species).

Shame feels "bad." It is an uncomfortable feeling that gives rise to self-deprecation and self-doubt. However, it is shame that enables humans to learn from interpersonal mistakes and develop the capacity for love and loving. It is shame that lies at the base of conscience and compassion. In a very real way, healthy human shame is nature's way of conditioning the human being to function adequately within a social context.

Origins of Shame: Natural

Developmental theory (another psychological theory) poses that there are stages of development common to all human beings. Each of these stages notes an apparent dual nature to the human experience, i.e., that people appear to be composed of two sides ("good" and "bad"), and that the quality of what is put in by others will affect the quality of the emerging person. In infancy, the child learns either trust or mistrust in relationship with the primary care-giver (usually the mother); therefore, a mother who does a good job of being available to the child throughout infancy will likely create a sense of trust within the child; whereas the mother who is negligent or unavailable during infancy helps to create a child who has a large amount of mistrust throughout his or her life.

Later, in toddlerhood, the young child begins to exhibit the basic personality structure that will exist throughout the child's life. Accompanying this personality structure are the emergent feelings of autonomy (joy of self) and shame (despair of self). These feelings represent the dual nature of the child's development as a toddler. Parents (both father and mother) who are aware of the developmental peculiarities of toddlerhood (see the discussion of separation, individuation, and differentiation, Chapter 2, page 10), and respond successfully to them are likely to produce children who experience emotionally satisfying lives; whereas parents who misunderstand the processes of toddlerhood are likely to engender a great deal more shame in the youngster than would be considered healthy. When this occurs, the character of the emerging person is apt to be highly affected by this over-abundance of shame, and the personality that results will be in some way become failure oriented. Usually, the greater the damage done in the early years, the sooner the failures will appear in the person's life.

Origins of Shame: Interpersonal

As noted earlier, shame is a natural part of being human and is experienced routinely and often by a developing child. However, the way a child's shame is handled by his caretakers is critical to the health of the resulting adult person. Most often, shame is triggered by some interpersonal event that usually involves some measure of failure. When there are two people present in a relationship and one of them experiences some aspect of the shame response, there will be a reciprocal response from the other.

For example, a three year old girl has just said a swear word in front of the minister at a wedding reception in the church's banquet room. The child may not be aware that the word she used was inappropriate, but the parent certainly knows this. The parent has an immediate shame response and becomes visibly embarrassed. Once this response has become real for the parent, it will next become part of the relationship between the parent and the child.

Consider the following possibilities: one parent might simply point out to the child that the word is not acceptable for use by children, another might chastise the child by scolding and demeaning her, another might try to excuse the behavior by stating that the child must be learning such things in daycare, another parent might strike the child, while still another will wait until they get out to the car and then try to instruct the child as to what she did wrong.

There are dozens of typical responses to such instances, yet it remains that the quality of the parent's response to a child's behavior will greatly influence the amount of shame experienced by the child. Clearly then, the way in which the parent disciplines the child in response to behavioral mistakes will affect the way the child feels about herself.

Corrective Shame

Shame has an adaptive function that serves to help people change various undesirable behaviors in relationship to their social context; simply put, shame is the essence of conscience. The human conscience is normally in place at about 42 months and appears to be the result of numerous shame and anger experiences on the part of the child which have been successfully and lovingly contained by the mother (and later, the father). As the toddler child struggles with strong internal forces of negativity (e.g., grandiosity entitlement, anger, and hate), the mother and father construct a world of emotional and physical safety that serves to teach the child that he is loved in spite of the negativity. As a result, the child ultimately loves mother and father in return, and internalizes this love in the form of conscience. This conscience is later transferred from the parents to the family (immediate and extended), and eventually from the family to the society as the child matures. (See Chapter 3 on conscience development; page 21 ff.)

Toxic Shame

The concept of toxic shame represented here is drawn from material presented by modern teacher and lecturer John Bradshaw.

In the most basic sense, toxic shame is an over-abundant amount of accumulated shame that poisons and hurts the individual (and those around him). Where healthy shame (conscience) leads a person to find a better way to interact or relate with other people, toxic shame leads a person to fail in close personal relationships. Toxic shame tends to result in a world of personal failure and unhappiness. Toxic shame lurks unseen (yet keenly sensed) in the dysfunctional family system and gives way to a conspiracy among the family members which keeps the shame alive, active, untouchable and most of all, hidden from the members of the system. In many ways, toxic shame is like a creature that takes over the emotional life of a family and will not allow success or happiness to exist in its presence. The concept of hell is representative of the spirit of persons enveloped in toxic shame.

For a better understanding of the concept of toxic shame, consider the following encapsulation of life in a family system that revolves around an alcoholic father.

> The father is the dominant figure in the family, but he drinks to excess and at times behaves in a way that embarrasses (shames) other family members. Anyone in the system who confronts dad about his drinking meets with stern denials, rationalizations, blame, guilt, or rage. In light of this dynamic, the less powerful members of the system learn to cope with their own strong feelings by ignoring and avoiding them. Very often, the people in an alcoholic family lose the ability to actually feel their own feelings, and the shame, rage, hate, despair, fear, and more go inward and downward into a kind of internal holding pattern, and emotional growth stops. These feelings remain buried until the freedom of adulthood (or divorce in the case of the wife) allows them to emerge, but since there has been no adequate "affective (i.e., feeling) education," they emerge in harmful and destructive ways, leaving the person to feel flawed and unworthy (more shame) as a result. Often, alcohol, sex, drugs, excitement, rage, depression, and other coping strategies are employed to kill the pain of the emerging feelings, and the cycle of despair and unhealthiness is perpetuated.

The above example illustrates what can and does happen in any number of family systems which are affected by the various forms of abuse and dysfunction that are present in our society and culture. It is up to each individual to find her own way to truly break the cycle that arises from the avoidance of the shame experience and the resulting complications.

A Model for Shame Recovery

The first step in any recovery effort is to accept the presence of a personal problem; when it comes to shame, this is not easy for most people, in that strong psychological denial of the existence of internal shame and the tendency to deny personal responsibility are often major factors in slowing the progress of a recovery.

Second, recovery involves accepting the premise that avoidance of shame motivates interpersonal defensive behaviors.

Third, listening to one's inner voice and hearing one's own "self talk" is necessary. Usually, most people will then be able to realize that they have been telling themselves "bad" things about themselves and then do "bad" things as a result.

Fourth, the message to the self must be changed. Begin to counter the harmful messages with useful and healthful ones. "I'm ok'" is probably the single most important self message to learn in a recovery effort.

Fifth, one must recognize that behavior is a choice and that choices are a result of will. The human personality serves to do two things: satisfy needs and protect the self against harm (emotional and physical). The quality of a person's character is measured by the manner (choices) in which he achieves those two functions.

Sixth, one must know that if one is going to change, one must believe that one *can* change. Last, is to live, make mistakes, learn, forgive, and repeat again and again.

A Footnote

Recovery from any kind of shame disorder will proceed much more efficiently and effectively when a person is willing to reach out for help from a treatment professional.

TIME-OUT: CONTROL IN A MINUTE (OR TWO)

A Parental Must for kids aged 3 to 6

Introduction

Time-out has come to be a staple in the arsenal of parenting techniques for at least the past two generations, and for the most part, time-out is an absolute must for parents who desire to teach their children self discipline and respect for others.

Time-out is to be used as a short-term response for undesirable behaviors (e.g., kicking, hitting, swearing, yelling, name-calling, etc.) in younger children. What follows is a template for standard time-out practices developed from years of experience with children and parents.

The intervention offered here is intended for use with children in the age range of three through six years; time-out can be used to about age twelve, but there are other, more effective interventions which can replace time-out as the child matures.

> *Time-out should not be used as a response for defiance or noncompliance. Win/Win Parenting is the preferred method for motivating a child toward compliance.*

Please note: The philosophy underlying this intervention does not generally classify defiance of parental authority as totally "bad." Defiance in children is seen as an expression of a desire for selfhood separate from parents. When handled effectively, defiance can be transformed into self-determination, ambition, and emotional commitment for goal attainment.

The overall purposeof time-out is for the child to learn that he can, indeed, submit to adult authority and ultimately demonstrate acceptable behavior in spite of the desire to do otherwise, and for the parent to learn to accomplish this without giving in to either her own or her child's anger.

Particulars

Before initiating this intervention, several variables need to be considered and solidified:

- *Length of the time-out period.* Fifteen seconds to two minutes. Use fifteen seconds to begin the intervention with three year-olds and work up to two minutes for four, five, and six year-olds. Extended periods of time-out are usually ineffective and self-defeating in that they represent parental anger and loss of control. (Time-out can and should be replaced with "Work as Punishment" (see below) at around ages six or seven.)

- *Location of the time-out area.* A chair or carpet square should be used as the time-out area. It should not be facing a corner (to reduce shaming), and should be in a room other than the child's bedroom (to allow for the bedroom as a fall-back measure).

- *Posture.* The child is expected to sit quietly, upright, and still with hands folded in the lap; eyes should be staring forward with legs either folded or with feet flat on the floor (depending upon use of carpet square or chair). Parental insistence upon exact compliance is imperative at this point for the intervention to be effective.

- *Timer.* The parent is the timekeeper; some visible timepiece can be helpful.

The Procedure

To begin, imagine that your child (a five year old boy in this case) is calling you a "big dummy" because you won't allow him a snack before dinner; you have politely and firmly instructed him to stop. He escalates his name calling and even taunts you to take action. This is a reasonable place to intervene with time-out (rather than spanking, threatening, taking toys away, or yelling).

Consider these factors:

- I*dentify the behavior and send him to time-out for the specified time (in this case one minute).* Do not warn; do not threaten.

  Note: Many parents question the effectiveness of using only one minute for time-out; many agree with lessons learned through other parenting programs that one minute per year of age should be applied.

  Experience has shown that one minute is *long enough* to give the child something to work at, while it is *short enough* to give the child pause in his resistance to completing the parent's request. It is helpful to remind an obstinate child that his time-out is "only for one minute," and the time he is wasting is his own.

- *Insist that he sit erect in the chair for one minute.*

  Do not hesitate to start the time over if he breaks from the expected posture, but *do not add more time* for non-compliance or disrespect. It might take upwards of half an hour to gain compliance when the time-out intervention is first implemented with an older child (as opposed to a three-year-old), but don't give up, and don't give in to your anger (this is where only one minute pays off); if you stand firm, the child will eventually give in.

  Note: For children younger than three years (but not much younger then 24 months), time-out can be achieved by holding the child to the chair and counting to ten or fifteen, and then releasing the child. Don't be surprised if the child laughs or finds the situation infuriating; eventually the child will learn to accept timeout as the consequence for undesirable behaviors. The parent can become more demanding of "quiet time-out" as the child matures.

- *Now let's say that your son (four or older) resists going to time-out* by being silly, refusing to sit still, getting surly, or by physically balking at the request. When this happens, you can send him to his room (See: *Go To —our Room,* page 141) until he decides to comply with time-out.

- *If he goes to his room but will not stay there without incident, then you must physically insure that he remains in the room* by going to the room and remaining there with him. *(Never lock a child in a room from the outside.)* It is likely he will want you to leave; at this point you can inform him you will leave as long as he remains in the room without further exits or fussing. He may remain there as long as it takes him to change his mind about time-out. When he is ready to attend to his time-out, he is permitted to come out and ask you for permission to do so.

- *If he simply physically resists going to the room, or refuses to remain there quietly, then you will have to intervene* to physically keep him there. If at this point he becomes violent, physically restrain him until he is calm (see *Holdings and Restraints,* page 14). When he is calm, instruct him to remain in the room for at least five minutes, and then have him come out to you and ask for permission to attend to his time-out. Then he may go to the chair as originally instructed. Do not add more time because of the necessity for restraint.

- *After he has completed the time-out period you should thank him;* parents need to remember that it can be humiliating for a child to give in, therefore, praise the good decision.

  Parents also need remember that it is the child's job to experience and display strong emotions; it is the parent's job to constrain these situations with reasonable authority.

- *Let go.* It will do no good whatsoever to revisit the incident with him at some later time. An exception to this recommendation would be for the parent who is willing to process the situation at a later time when the child and parent are in a different place (e.g., on the way to the store, a game, or taking him to visit a friend). Remember: children learn how to behave by experiencing parental (i.e., adult) behaviors; they rarely learn to change behavior from words alone.

Keep in mind these essential elements of time-out:

- The parent must show confidence
- The parent must remain calm
- The child must comply

When a large dollop of love and understanding is applied to the firmness of the time-out procedure, the developing child learns to adhere to the rules of the family while experiencing the acceptance and compassion of the wise parent.

A Final Note

Time-out and the other interventions recommended in this procedure can be applied with or without clinical assistance at the discretion of the parent. However, if you are experiencing numerous and various forms of misbehavior from your children, then contact a therapist or counselor who specializes in working with children and parents. **Please note: therapy and counseling work best for children under 16 when the counselor or therapist works equally with the parents.**

GO TO YOUR ROOM: ANOTHER PARENTAL MUST

Introduction

It is often necessary for parents to "reset" situations with their children, especially when time-out seems to be failing, or when a child seems to be out of control (e.g., temper losses, extensive arguing, and/or disrespect for rights of others). *Go To ~~o~~ur Room* is an extremely valuable tool for effective parenting through a child's first thirteen years ***(this intervention is not developmentally suited for children younger than about three years).***

There are many musts in parenting and child rearing, and one of the more important is for a child to go to the bedroom when instructed to do so by a parent. It is of the utmost importance to master this intervention early in a child's life; the longer a parent waits to employ this tool, the harder it will be to achieve success.

The Set-up

Imagine that you have sent your six year-old child to time-out and he has refused to go, or has fooled around to the point that you can see he's not going to comply. This is the time to send him to his room with the command: "Go to your room and stay there for at least five minutes and then when you are ready to complete your time-out, find me and ask for my permission to go to time-out."

An older child might be resisting the completion of a chore, or refusing to stop name calling, or fighting with a sibling. No matter. It is perfectly reasonable to send a child to her room when a parent believes that the child should have her freedoms restricted, either for a specified length of time (for some punishable offense), or until compliance for a given task has been obtained by the parent.

The Terms

When you tell a child to go to the bedroom until he decides to comply with a request ("time-out" in above example), the final word regarding the restriction to the room still resides with you, yet the child has the choice as to the length of time he will spend there. If the child stays in his room, then comes out, seeks your permission, and ultimately finishes the time-out as prescribed without incident, then the intervention is over and nothing further needs to be said. If not, you need only make sure that the child stays there.

If your child refuses to go to the room as asked, you can physically usher him into the room. If there is violent resistance, then you can move on to physical restraint (See *Holdings and Restraints,* page 143).

When implementing *Go To –our Room* with an older, larger child, a parent may have to withhold various privileges until the child ultimately complies with the request (see "Demanding" in *Variations on Win/Win Parenting,* page 163). Parents should do everything in their power to maintain control over their own anger when attempting to apply disciplinary techniques with their child, and remember one primary fact: *A parent does not have control over a child's behaviors; parents control only themselves and the environment.*

If the child goes to the room, but comes out of the room without complying to the assigned conditions for ending the time in the room, he should be sent back until compliance is obtained. If the child has been sent to the bedroom for a specified time period and comes out for any reason, then he should be sent back to the room and the time restarted from zero (do not add more time).

If the child refuses to remain in the room, then action can be taken to prevent him from exiting the room. This is especially important for smaller children aged twelve and under. The child can be ushered back to the room and the parent can remain with him. It is a good idea to close the door behind and remain near the door. It is likely that a child will protest the parent's presence in the room; if this is the case, he can be assured the parent will leave the room if he pledges to remain in the room with no further incident. If agreement is given, then the parent can exit and await compliance. When compliance is given, the intervention ends and the child is praised for making a good decision. If he continues to goad or taunt after having made an agreement to comply, the parent can go back and remain in the room. If the child's anger escalates, restraint should be employed (See: *Holdings and Restaints,* page 143).

Once a child has given his cooperation and stays in the room; it must be remembered that the intervention is not over until compliance ..ith the original request is supplied by the child.

Conclusion

The use of Time-out, Go To Your Room, and Physical Restraint are the three elements of teaching a child the very basics of childhood. Many parents want their children to be happy and unstressed, but many forget that it is the nature of children to argue, complain, resist authority, vie for power and act immaturely. Effective parents must often withstand the pain of having their children angry with them in the short-term for doing what is right for them in the long-term.

The Last Resort

This intervention is intended for use by parents who seek help in handling their children's worst behaviors. The procedures outlined below will work for most children and parents in most situations. These methods are far better than spanking, yelling, physically man-handling, or threatening children into obedience.

This intervention is specifically designed to help parents find a better way to handle their children's raging (out of control) behaviors. Holdings and restraints are performed only with children who are small enough to be safely held; larger, older children need to be handled with different methods which often require professional direction and supervision.

Parents who feel uncomfortable hearing their children yell and scream should seek professional assistance before employing the interventions included in this intervention. Holdings and restraints are designed to respond to a child's worst behaviors and most difficult feelings; there will be extreme experiences of anger, hate, pain, sadness and even violence. Further, many parents will not hold or restrain their children long enough to achieve true resolution and thus will create even more difficult situations for the future. Expert assistance is the best way to proceed with the material that follows.

Parents wishing to learn about holding theory and holding techniques should obtain a copy of the book *Holding Time* by Martha Welch.

> ***If you are a parent seeking help ..ith a very difficult child (aged 12 and under) read this entire section and seek professional assistance. Be sure to inquire as to ..hether your therapist has an a..areness of holding techniques and kno..s ho...to help you employ them.***

Holding

A holding, per Dr. Welch, is a shared experience between a parent and a child in which the child must surrender total control and authority to the parent. This situation is reflective of recreating the mother-child relationship of infancy.

Parent-initiated holdings create a situation in which the child becomes, at first, very uncomfortable and resistant to the idea of being held. The child is confined and restricted from freedom and has lost virtually all physical freedoms save those that can be enjoyed while restrained. Usually children will begin to complain that they hurt or that they feel sick and need to be left alone; often children will use any number of manipulations to get the parent to surrender to her will to be set free of the holding.

Holdings differ from restraints (see below) in that they are done on somewhat of a schedule, more or less as a matter of course in the child's routine with the parent. Holdings should be conducted when plenty of time is available for the parent and the child to complete the experience.

Physical Restraint

Physical restraint is employed when lesser interventions (e.g., *Time-out*, page 137, *Go To Your Room*, page 141) appear to fail; restraints are employed to stop a child from leaving a given environment, or to stop a child from destructive and self-destructive behaviors. *Note: never restrain a child because she will not comply with a task or command* (except the command to remain in her room, or the request to stop some sort of destructive, out of control behavior).

Physical restraints will often be required in the early stages of therapies where parents learn new and effective parenting techniques; here the child must test the parent's resolve regarding "new found" parenting techniques (this is why knowledgeable therapists often warn that things will get worse before they get better). Physical restraints should be employed only after a parent or caretaker is taught the best ways to therapeutically restrain and contain a raging child.

> ***Note: A raging child has no sense of ..hat is rational; parents should al..ays expect the unexpected. Never assume safety; al..ays plan safety. A raging child ..ill try to hurt a parent and might try to hurt herself. Get expert counseling and restraint training from a professional before employing a restraint at home.***

What to expect

Whether exercising a holding, or employing a restraint, it is almost guaranteed that a child will fight a parent's efforts to hold her, so it is usually a good idea to expect a great deal of resistance. Some therapists will teach parents how to employ a "basket hold," while others might teach a parent to "swaddle" a child so that the child can hurt neither herself or the parent. Swaddling can be very useful for allowing a parent greater freedom to address problems with eye contact, spitting, and head banging in the holding/restraint experience.

As noted in *Holding Time,* holdings and restraints will proceed in three distinct phases: confrontation, protestation, and resolution. A child will manifest his control issues in a variety of ways to get the parent to stop the holding, thus allowing the child to regain control and freedom.

Parents must continue the holding until some connection is occurring that transcends compliance and control issues. The reason for doing a holding or restraint with a child is *not* merely to get the child to stay in the room; it is to get the child to a point inside himself where he is honestly willing to comply with parental demands because the child feels better.

In order for a child to feel better in a situation such as mentioned here, the child will have to expel a great deal of venomous rage in a safely contained manner (the parent's embrace), remain in that embrace until the rage has passed, and then reconcile with the parent in softness and love. Sometimes when pressed for time, a parent might have to settle for mere compliance, but in the long run, parent and child must experience a reconnection with one another in a loving way; this is where the conscience and guilt (rapprochement) will be forged.

Holdings and restraints can produce very powerful results. In many cases a successful experience will leave both the parent and the child emotionally drained yet feeling very close to one another. It is at this point that a child learns that he is a good person in spite of bad behaviors. This is one of those times when a parent's behavior will actually teach a child that it is possible for the parent to hate the behavior, but love the child.

Also, parents should be careful after holdings to resist the temptation to be "extra nice" to the child; instead, they should allow for the child to be "extra nice" to them. It must always be remembered that the relationship between a parent and child is a power-oriented relationship, especially for the child; parents should do their level best to remain steady for their children in times of intense emotional experiences, proving the child to be less than all powerful, yet providing a platform for reconciliation (and atonement).

After resolution (reconciliation) has occurred, or after the parent has decided that enough is enough, discuss with your child what is required once the holding is over. If the holding was initiated as a result of a failed time-out (i.e., restraint), then inform the child that he must retrace the steps that led to the holding (go backward from remaining in the room to the initial time-out). The child will be released from the restraint, remain in the room for a short while, seek out the parent and ask to sit in time-out, sit in time-out, and finally receive praise for making a good decision. At this point, the intervention is over and it is time to get on with life. For those parents who used holding because the child would not stay in her room for a prescribed time, the issue is closed when the child completes the time without incident.

If a holding has been completed, and the child fails to comply with the prior requests, the child did not achieve resolution in the holding and will most likely have to re-experience the holding/restraint process until resolution is revealed by way of compliance.

In the end, successful resolutions to numerous holdings and restraints will result in a rejuvenation of the bond between the child and the parent. It is likely that children will continue to verbally resist holdings and restraints, yet they will persist in committing acts and behaviors which will require the use of restraint as the only viable response to the situation. Parents should not stop holdings because they feel manipulated into performing them; rather they should continue to use them to address the manipulations and continue to work the child toward her anger, through the anger, and toward resolution with parental love.

> ***Remember: ..ork ..ith a professional. Help is needed to resist the parental traps of anger, despair, and the desire to blame and punish the child.***

GROUNDING

Grounding is a punishment and therefore needs to be used judiciously and sparingly. To ground a child is to restrict him to the house or to the bedroom. Grounding usually means that the child has lost all freedoms for the duration of the grounding period.

Ineffective Grounding

Many parents find that grounding is a consequence or punishment that loses its effectiveness after a period of success. There are specific reasons that grounding fails to alter future infractions of various rules. A few of those reasons follow:

- *Overuse.* Grounding a child to her room or the house is a relatively easy thing for a parent to do. It requires little thought and provides an instantaneous unpleasant situation for the wayward child. When it is used as the primary tool for handling parenting problems, it will lose its effectiveness due to the anger that will result within the child. The child will become resentful and disrespectful of the parent, and will then act worse to get back at the parent.

- *Misuse.* When a parent grounds a child for an indefinite period of time, or when the child is grounded for a specified but prolonged interval (weeks or months), the intervention loses its meaning because most parents will not enforce the grounding for the entire period. If they do, they find that the child "goes crazy" when released.

- *Abuse.* Many parents develop an affinity for grounding when they are angry, and angry behaviors are generally considered abusive. Very often, the angry parent will impose grounding in situations where it is not fitting to do so simply because he is so angry with the child that the parent wants to hurt the child, to "teach a lesson."

> *Remember: never "ground" a child for a given period of time because he will not comply with a given demand; "ground" the child until he is prepared to comply with the task at hand; time limited "groundings" are punishments, not motivators.*

For instance, a twelve year old boy who will not mow the lawn will not be motivated to do so as a result of a weekend's worth of grounding; in fact it will be more likely that he will either wait out the period, get angry (and get even) or manipulate his way out of it.

Effective Grounding

Grounding is effective when used in two distinctly different situations.

First, when a child has committed some offense against another person or has broken a major rule, grounding may be in order. Usually, grounding should be reserved as a response for violating freedoms (curfew, speech, whereabouts). A child who has violated curfew, or has violated rules about whereabouts, can be grounded for a specified period (rarely more than a couple of days). See *Curfew Violations,* page 164.

Second, grounding can be effective in situations involving noncompliance. In these cases the child can be grounded to the room or home *until* a specified job or task is completed (see "Demanding" in

Variations on Win/Win Parenting, page 163). This is not a contradiction of what was stated earlier regarding ineffective grounding, in that the length of the restriction is in the control of the youngster. This technique should be used sparingly.

Examples of Groundable Infractions

- *Swearing.* No more than an hour.
- *Name calling.* No more than an hour.
- *Curfew.* No more than two days.
- *Destruction of property.* One or two days (up to one week) with the provision of reparation (e.g., compensation for or repair of damage).
- *Alcohol.* One week
- *Alcohol and driving.* One month
- *Marijuana.* Until urine is clean
- *School suspensions.* Throughout suspension, if over weekend, include weekend

Conclusion

Grounding has become one of the more popular behavioral interventions in our society today. On the whole, grounding can be an effective tool for setting and maintaining a variety of limits. Care must be taken to avoid using this tool as the primary response for all behavioral difficulties. Parents must remember that a hammer is a useful tool for building a home; it is not, however, the only one.

WORK AS "PUNISHMENT" (6 THROUGH 17)

Many parents struggle to find alternatives to grounding as responses to unwanted behaviors. It is important that a parent remembers that punishments are designed to provide a consequence for a past behavior and a deterrent for future unwanted similar behavior.

What to do? Consider *work.*

Kids hate it; parents wish they could get more of it.

Procedure

When a youngster does something that is undesirable (name calling, swearing, hitting, destroying property, skipping school, etc.), give him something to do; something that is not desirable; something that will cause the child to give pause the next time a similar situation arises.

Parents have a number of jobs, tasks and chores that can be used as punishments for bad behaviors. Consider the following:

- Sweeping the garage
- Scrubbing the garage floor
- Cleaning toilets and bathrooms
- Cleaning beneath the kitchen sink
- Cleaning windows
- Washing and vacuuming the car
- Cleaning the family room
- Doing the family's laundry
- Scrubbing the deck
- Painting a room
- Cleaning the oven
- Shampooing rugs and carpets
- Raking leaves
- Mowing the lawn
- Shoveling snow

These are just a few of the things that parents can use as responses and deterrents for various unwanted behaviors. And remember, just because a job was done on Monday, doesn't mean it can't be reassigned on Wednesday; the point is to get the child doing the work. The manner of work is not as important as the fact that it is a chore and is disliked by the child.

Backup plan

What about the child who refuses to do the work?

Work is something that children tend to avoid like the plague, and they show a great deal of resistance to both starting and completing job assignments. This is where the old standby, *grounding,* can come back into favor.

If a youngster decides that she will not complete an assigned task, then place the child on restriction until the job is completed. This means no TV, no telephone, no music, and no visits from friends until the work is completed. The amount of time that the child is restricted is totally in his control.

It is important to pay attention to the age and developmental abilities of the child in question. It is unreasonable to expect that a seven-year old boy would be able to scrub the garage floor, or have a ten-year old girl paint the living room.

Early use of this intervention will yield conditions in which later use will be less difficult.

Rationale

Many undesirable behaviors are unwittingly encouraged by a parent who will scold, chastise, demean, or yell at the child, but do little else. After a while the child learns that when he does something wrong, the worst that will happen will be a few moments of emotional discomfort due to the parent's tirade. Although such a parental response is considered to be somewhat abusive, this is not much for a child to have to pay for doing something wrong, and it is likely that the child will do it again, if for no other reason than to anger the parent.

Applying work to these situations and removing parental emotion from the equation creates an unpleasant consequence that becomes a fact of the child's life; the child's freedoms will not be restored until the successful completion of the job. When a parent employs this strategy on a consistent basis, the child becomes conditioned to expect a work assignment, and he will begin to make choices based on this reality rather than adopting the common attitude of "My mother's going to kill me for this, but what the heck...."

Do This

Think about your child for a few moments and choose an undesirable behavior that she commits on a somewhat regular basis. Look around the house and make some notes in your mind regarding things that need to be done. The next time your child commits an infraction, assign one of those jobs. Follow the procedure noted above.

Try it; you'll like it.

SIBLING RIVALRY

For simplicity's sake this section is written as though sibling rivalry occurs between two children only; this is, however, not always the case. Sibling rivalry can occur among any number of children in a family system. Also note, this section is written for family systems in which there are two parents. Single parents can certainly benefit from the material, but should consider the aspects of splitting (see Chapter 7, pg. 91) when going over it. When single parents internally "split" their children as good and bad, and then treat them as good and bad, the fires of sibling rivalry will be well stoked.

What is Sibling Rivalry?

Most parents are not granted the opportunity of raising only one child at a time and are many times destined to struggle with the ongoing conflicts that seem to continually arise when there is more than one child in a family.

Sibling rivalry is a process of interaction that occurs between siblings. It is manifested by continual bickering and arguing that takes place between the children. It is also revealed in ongoing criticism, mocking, verbal and physical abuse, and one child belittling another. There is usually one who is the stronger of the two and the other who appears the weaker and thus, the victim. This is the simple definition.

A closer look into situations of sibling rivalry usually reveals that more is involved than two children who are continually at odds with one another. In almost all cases there is a set of parents who are at odds over how to handle the rivalry, or a single parent who is internally torn over which child is right and which is wrong. What these parents don't seem to realize is that by their efforts to resolve their children's conflicts, they are revealing that they cannot resolve their own. Usually, the very struggle that is occurring between the children is a reflection of the struggle taking place within the parent(s).

A more complete definition for sibling rivalry incorporates an entire family system that is at odds with one another, where the children are acting out the rivalry that exists within the parent(s). A broader perspective of sibling rivalry includes the concept of family rivalry, where each member in the system is struggling to assert his individuality in relationship to the others in the system by trying to assert himself as "right." The aggressor always has some reason for wounding the victim; the victim is always justified in desiring relief from the aggressor by way of the grace of the rescuer (a parent).

Where to Start

First and foremost, parents need to admit they need help with their children. They must, however, acknowledge that each must make some change that will be instrumental in making adjustments to the way the family operates. The major drawback with this premise is that each parent is able to see the problems as they exist in the other, but resist acknowledging and changing flaws within him- or herself. Thus, to achieve true resolution, each parent must look inward and make the changes that are necessary for addressing problems in a more cooperative fashion. This is usually a very difficult task in that "old habits die hard," especially ones that are deeply buried within a person's psyche.

Once parents are willing to acknowledge that they must change and begin exercising those changes, they are ready to work at dealing with their children.

The chief reason for failure in a sibling rivalry situation is that there is some question as to who is right and who is wrong. For the most part, this notion must cease. There will be times when a parent will see something that will warrant a punishment for only one child, but these occasions are few in comparison to the number of times that a parent will not clearly know what has actually occurred between children.

Therefore, parents must change their assumptions about what they think is happening between their children. It is important that parents are able to assume that both of the children are a fault in most situations. Parents need to remember that it is as unhealthy to promote victimhood as it is to promote aggression, since victimhood promotes its own unhealthy way to achieve power.

Parents must learn to refrain from rescuing and judging, and to move toward a more unbiased view of what is going on.

Address the Noise

One of the safest ways to handle rivalry is for the parents to agree with one another that episodes of sibling rivalry are viewed as disturbances or disruptions in the peace of the family that involves both (or all) of the children. Thus if Johnny and Billy are quarreling over who has rights to a particular toy, they should be separated from one another for a specified period of time (fifteen minutes for example) ***for making noise.*** Parent(s) should refrain from attempting to settle the argument, but if the item in question clearly belongs to one child or the other, then the parent(s) can choose to return that item to its rightful owner, but still maintain the period of separation. Use of this strategy will give both children the message that they are responsible for the outcome of their interactions regardless of who is right and who is wrong, and will give neither of them more power than the other.

Be Preemptive Regarding Possible Future Argument

Another important intervention is "pre-use" division or assignment of ownership. Often, parents are forced to buy items that must be considered community property. Things such as televisions, video games, computers, and the like are not usually given to one child or the other, but are given jointly. When this is the case, parents should be careful to lay out the rules for use prior to giving the item to the children. When rules are outlined in advance (they should be written down and amended as needed), these rules

can be enforced uniformly regardless of which child is being co
any one time.

For instance, Johnny and Billy get a new video game app
Christmas. Each should be assigned times for individual use, and
joint use. If the rules for joint use are violated (i.e., fighting, nam
swearing, arguing) then both lose the opportunity to play for a
time (e.g., the rest of the evening), regardless who has individu
on the schedule. If one is playing during his allotted time and inv
brother to play, and later decides to ask his brother to leave, then he
have the right to do so, as long as he is respectful and well behaved
exchange. Parents who are able to communicate and cooperate wit
another will usually be able to come up with a system that will work
applied uniformly and consistently.

Another way around this dilemma is to refrain from buying joi
owned items for the children. Parents can buy large ticket items
themselves and allow the children to use them at their discretion accordi
to guidelines as noted above. Things such as individual CD's, DVD's, a
computer games can be given to each child as fits the child's dispositio
and tastes, but the right to use the device that operates the item in questio
remains in the parents' realm of authority. As long as rules for use ar
followed and cooperation is in effect, the kids can use the equipment; when
rules are broken, consequences can flow as noted above.

Ownership

Another aspect of resolving rivalry situations is the idea of ownership. Personal items such as clothes, shoes, socks, toys, games and such should be granted to each child individually. They should be labeled in such a way as to be discernible one from the other. All arguments over such items are resolved along the lines of ownership. Thus, any argument over an individual's item can be settled merely by checking the item to see to whom it belongs. If the situation results in noise, the children can be separated for short while, but the item is still returned to its rightful owner.

Once ownership has been declared, sharing is allowed with consent, but can be revoked without cause unless the revocation creates an undue hardship. For instance, Johnny allows Billy to borrow his sweatshirt to wear to school and then gets angry with Billy before leaving for the bus. If there is enough time to give back the sweatshirt, Billy must do so; if they are at school and Johnny gets angry at Billy in gym class, he can't demand that Billy give him the sweatshirt until they get home from school.

y one of the more important aspects of : honored regardless of the parent's attitudes ts think that children should share with one when a parent insists that sharing overrides

ignty are two of the very basic elements of our in the home is to invite heightened contention aring is taught by parents who are willing to share able to point out that sharing can be a rewarding e giver or receiver. It should be remembered that share are children who are likely to feel a lack of or ownership within themselves; they become stingy ow feel deprived. It is better to seek out the source of ivation, rather than to insist that a child share when she do so.

Separation and individuality

e: Throughout this section various references have been ade to individuality and separation. Both are important spects of healthy character development.

e primary response to occurrences of sibling rivalry should be to te the children from one another, and thus allow them to decide if want to spend time together by the behaviors they choose when they together. This can always be the parent's fall-back position, if for no her reason than to give the parent time to think about the situation at and. The process of separating the children one from another is the best way to foster independent thinking and personal responsibility.

Individuality is the logical result of effective separation. A person's sense of self (and self-worth) is a very important aspect of being alive. Depression, anxiety, and various other emotional difficulties can be usually be traced back to a person's inability to feel like a separate and complete human being.

Sibling rivalry is a reflection not only of a child's lack of self-worth, but rather a lack of self-worth throughout the family system. As with so many other behavioral and emotional difficulties, resolution comes from within each person, with the parent(s) leading the way.

RIDING IN CARS WITH NOISE

A common complaint of many parents has to do with th children sometimes behave in the car. At these times, many pare scold their children while driving and consequently add to the n their own anger and frustration. A very simple response to such is to pull over, stop the car and wait for the child or children to ge

When a parent pulls off to the side of the road, an entirely r different set of circumstances is created for the children in that t be subject to the will of the parent(rather than the other way ar because the parent can announce that the car will not move again u noise stops. Sitting in a parked car gets old very quickly and in mos the children will be motivated to get moving again.

It is important that parents remember they control the environ (the car) and the children control their behavior (the noise). When th is at a stop, a Win/Win situation is constructed (see *Win/Win: the Bus of Parenting,* page 156) in which the car will move when the children quiet. The parent doesn't have to do anything but sit there and wait for children to tire of their own predicament and thus be motivated to com with the parent's desire for civility in the car.

Many parents will ask, "What if we are on our way to someplac important and I don't have time to pull over and wait?" A second questio provides the answer: "How safe is it to drive a car when distracted by noisy and out of control children" or "what's more important, getting there on time or being safe?" Usually, the destination is not as important as the child's knowledge that the car will not move until quiet has been restored.

The following example illustrates how the intervention works (or doesn't work):

> A parent educator had presented the parked car intervention to a group of parents and was doing a follow-up of the outcomes the next week. Several of the parents in the class noted that they had achieved success very quickly, but one set of parents indicated that the intervention did not work for them. The instructor quickly replied, "Then you shouldn't be sitting here right now." The parents, somewhat taken aback by this comment, defensively asked "Why not?" The instructor's reply was stunning in its simplicity, "Because the terms of the intervention state that the car does not move until quiet is restored; therefore, if you had followed the intervention to the letter, and it didn't work, you should be parked alongside

pulled over."

rvention that failed, but rather the parents who en.

ps for implementation

to use this intervention, be sure that time is on ıp failure by using it when in a hurry.

ntion when on the way to a place of favor for the vention will be very difficult to employ if used on desired destination, especially in the early going.

ıt of the ignition. This will eliminate the likelihood act on the part of an angry impulsive child.

ervention is employed, there is only one way for it to ence.

SS OF PARENTING

Win/Win Parenting

e from children is most often regarded as negative by adults, quently, children are often punished by an angry parent. The ı outcome of this style of parenting is rigid authoritarianism and ıed creativity. However, when a parent learns to regard defiance ıanifestation of self-determination, the parent can reconstruct t situations into learning experiences that have far-reaching positive omes.

One method for achieving this reconstructive process is called Win/ n Parenting. The long-term outcome of this style of parenting is "free ıinking" and creativity, with an awareness of potential consequences for ı given behavior. If applied consistently, this style of parenting will be effective for children from late toddlerhood through late adolescence.

What is Win/Win Parenting?

Win/Win Parenting is a technique employed by a parent that creates a winning environment for a child. Win/Win situations are those in which both parties can win. This model for parenting closely resembles the arbitration of contracts in the business world, except here, the parent uses his authority to maintain control over the range of the contract. In other words, the parent will allow for freedom of choice, but will retain the authority to determine various outcomes (see *Win/Win Parenting Worksheet,* page 160).

How Does It Work?

Consider the parent of an older teenage boy who is lazy, but likes to have the car on Friday evenings to entertain his girlfriend. On Thursday afternoon the boy is asked to mow the grass, and he assures the parent he'll do it. His tone is surly and noncommittal, and the parent suspects that he'll put it off until anger and meanness become active in the interchange. The teen agreed with the request only to get his parent "off his back," but the parent knows this and realizes conflict is imminent. This is a common occurrence in many exchanges between children and parents in our society.

When he does put off the chore, there exists the makings of a very nasty interchange between parent and teen, or there exists the opportunity to employ a highly effective and positive Win/Win strategy. The situation becomes Win/Win when the parent puts off dealing with the grass until Friday afternoon when the boy comes and asks for the car. At this point, the parent simply states: "Yes, you may use the car after you mow the grass." The parent can also add: "Check the oil, inspect the tires, and fill the gas tank." The teen is now faced with a dilemma: he can comply with the parent's requests or face the unpleasant task of telling his girlfriend that he won't have a car for their date.

The truly beautiful thing about this scenario is that the teenager has to do all of his thinking without the parent saying another word. The parent doesn't have to be angry or threatening; he simply has to be firm in his insistence that he will withhold the car until his son has complied with the terms of the contract.

> ***It is important to let go of the notion that a parent's requests and demands must be met the moment they are issued. There are relatively fe... instances ..here immediate compliance is necessary for effective parenting.***

It is likely that situations will occur where a child might choose to forgo her original intent; in other words, she might decide that the privilege isn't worth the price. In these situations, be careful to avoid upping the ante in an effort to coerce compliance. The fact that the child has accepted parental terms is compliance enough. Further, sometimes the only way a teen can say "No" to peers is to set up a situation between himself and the parents in which the child appears to lose. Parents need to be patient, and not push. Stick to the contract; another chance will come later.

How Doesn't It Work?

There are two situations which appear to be Win/Win situations, but are truly not. The first is when a parent bribes a youngster into compliance. For example: "Amy, I will give you five dollars if you clean my car for me before noon today." Although this sounds like a good deal to the parent, it can be a losing situation because Amy might not need money and she might be more motivated to do something else with her time. In general people will do things when they are motivated to do so.

The second situation is when a parent *threatens* a child into compliance. An example of this would be: "If you don't clean that car right now, you will not be allowed to go to the dance on Thursday evening." This can appear to be a Win/Win situation to an angry parent, but it will not appear to be so to a teenaged boy or girl. Avoid the pitfalls of bribery and threatening, and work to use Win/Win Parenting in a spirit of mutual respect and recognition of personal sovereignty.

Patience and Wisdom

The effectiveness of Win/Win parenting strategies is grounded in patience and wisdom.

Patience means learning to wait until later to deal with something that is very pressing (to the parent) right now; *wisdom* means anticipating and planning the consequences of waiting instead of acting immediately.

An astronaut was given the following dilemma: "You have ten seconds to make a life or death decision. What would you do?" Without hesitation the astronaut replied, "I'd think for nine seconds and act in the tenth."

Win/Win parenting requires that a parent replace the tendency to punish a child for noncompliance with a genuine effort to allow nature to run its course in response to a child or teen's behavioral choices. Further, if it is true that children learn more from what parents do than what they say, then it stands to reason that if parents model patience and wisdom, patience and wisdom will be learned.

Steps to Win/Win Parenting

Getting effective results with Win/Win parenting can be accomplished if the parent is willing to follow a consistent pattern of behaviors. What follows is a generalized version of the technique:

- Make a request. It's okay to ask.
- Expect, anticipate, and accept resistance and refusal. It's okay to to be refused.
- Wait for the moment of leverage. This is when the youngster comes to you for something that she cannot achieve without your assistance or blessing.
- At the moment of leverage, state the verbal contract. "Yes, you may,...when you...."
- Stand your ground. Don't give in on your side of the contract. The only way for the parent to lose is to give in at this point.
- Calmly withstand the initial flurry of objections, complaints, and accusations.
- Have confidence in your child's ability to make the "right" choice for himself.
- Remember to say "Thank you." Compliance and cooperation are gifts; accept them graciously.

Potential Outcomes

Consistent use of strategies based in a Win/Win philosophy will greatly increase the chances that a child will comply with parental requests in a timely and cooperative manner. It is important that a parent moves away from the "Because I said so" mind-set, and moves toward a structured effort to develop a spirit of cooperation.

It is vital to remember that children are people, and that they have needs for power and control, just like grownups. Win/Win Parenting, if properly employed, will help produce children who will be more likely to think before they act, because we, their parents, learned to do the same.

Related Topics

Variations on Win/Win (page 161); *Motivation, Consequence, and Punishment* (page 126).

WIN/WIN PARENTING WORKSHEET

Thinking Is Easier Than Fighting

It seems that children live in a constant state of need and that parents, particularly mothers, feel responsible to fulfill those needs. Often, a major complaint from many parents is that they feel "ripped off" by their children (again, especially mothers who do many things for their children only to be refused by their children after making the simplest requests or demands). Win/Win Parenting is a way to avoid the pitfalls of the anger and guilt trap, which is so often set by our children.

What follows is a simple worksheet that will help parents think about what is going on between them and their children. When filling out the worksheet, remember that there are five basic areas of childhood dependency (and thus, parental authority): freedom, money, communication, entertainment, and food.

A. List ten things that are needs or desires brought to you by your child on a routine basis. Prioritize them according to the importance your child places on them.

1. ______________________________

2. ______________________________

3. ______________________________

4. ______________________________

5. ______________________________

6. ______________________________

7. ______________________________

8. ______________________________

9. ______________________________

10. ______________________________

B. List ten things that you would like for your child to perform on a routine basis. Prioritize them according to the importance you place on them.

1. ____________________
2. ____________________
3. ____________________
4. ____________________
5. ____________________
6. ____________________
7. ____________________
8. ____________________
9. ____________________
10. ____________________

Complete this sentence. Supply items from sections A and B respectively, matching selections by rank)

Yes, you may (or yes, I will) __________ when you __________ .
A B

You now have the makings of a Win/Win situation; Win/Win Parenting requires thought, practice, and patience. Many parents find it hard to think about what they are doing "all the time," but it is truly much easier over the long haul to learn that thinking clearly wins out over fighting and arguing.

VARIATIONS ON WIN/WIN PARENTING

As noted in the previous section, Win/Win techniques can be employed in a variety of situations that reflect accompanying parental attitudes, expectations, and preferences. What follows are several modifications for use of Win/Win strategies in different situations.

Magic
(use about 50% of the time)

Parents agree that it is pure magic for their kids to do things without being asked. Here's a way to do it: The least intrusive use of Win/Win strategies is when a parent notes that there is something that needs to be done by the child, but refrains from making a demand until the child wants something. This version of Win/Win Parenting truly reflects the benign nature of the Win/Win philosophy and most readily conveys the realtionship between freedom and responsibility.

For example, consider the parent of a senior toddler (about age four) who would like the toddler to pick up her blocks. Rather than ask the child outright to pick up the blocks, the parent can wait until the child asks the parent to pour a glass of milk, tie a shoe, fix a snack, etc.; the parent simply agrees to gratify the child after she picks up the blocks. Nothing further needs be said.

If the child meets the request, the child is gratified by the parent; if not, the parent just goes on without meeting the child's "need." The child is then left to figure out a way to get her need met without the parent's assistance. This added dimension is useful for teaching independence and limits.

If the child tries to meet the need without the parent and fails, then she may learn to choose differently the next time, or she may decide to come back to the parent and make a second request (this time more willing to cooperate with the parent).

If the child gains gratification without parental intervention, then autonomy and independence have been achieved; if the child finds she needs the mother or father to gain gratification, cooperation will be exercised. These are good things for both parent and child.

Remember, if a parent waits long enough, a child will always get into a situation that requires parental assistance; it is at this point that parental demands and requests have the greatest chance of being met.

Asking (use about 40% of the time)

Contrary to what many people have said about parenting in the past, there is nothing wrong with asking a youngster to complete a given task. Asking implies choice, and choice is an important reality in every decision whether that of an adult or a youngster.

When a parent sees something that needs be done by a child, the parent can certainly ask, and even remember to say "Please." Yet the parent needs be sure to expect, anticipate, and accept the fact that, initially, a child may resist or refuse to comply with the request.

As a matter of fact, parents need to view refusal as a challenge to be overcome.

Learn to Wait

In most cases, parents need to learn to give up the old notion that compliance needs to be immediate. Often, the desire for immediate compliance will backfire on the parent, and the parent will find himself in an uproar created by the child's passivity. Parents need to put aside the need for immediate compliance when feasible, and wait for the youngster to approach for assistance or "blessing" for some unrelated matter. At that point the parent says: "Yes," but with the addition of a second word: "...when."

Most parents tend to deny a child's want (or need) because the child has not complied with some earlier parental request. This is punishment, which gives rise to anger, resentment, shame, and self-defeatism. Punishment fails to teach the lessons that parents want their children to learn. For the most part, punishment is a way for a parent to vent anger and resentment toward the child.

Usually, when a parent is mindful of what she expects from her child or adolescent, use of a Win/Win strategy will result in a cooperative response from the youngster. The parent need only stand firm and execute the terms of the contract; most kids will do the right thing.

Demanding (use less often than 10%)

Usually, this is the part of Win/Win Parenting that attracts the most attention from parents. This variation focuses on the more coercive aspects of Win/Win Parenting strategies. It should be remembered that this aspect of the philosophy will engender hard feelings and should be used sparingly.

Parents often find themselves in situations where their child will refuse to comply with a request that the parent sees as requiring immediate atention. When the parent insists that compliance be immediate, there is no guarantee that a child will accommodate and resistance often becomes the norm.

If a parent wishes to make an immediate demand, he need only remove the child's freedoms until the child agrees to complete the task. Use phrases such as, "You're grounded until…," or "Go to your room until you decide to…." It's that simple. The task may not be completed immediately, but the consequence for failing to do so will be immediate and will last as long as the child refuses to comply with the assigned task.

Consider the following example: a teenage boy refuses to sweep the garage as requested. The parent is fed up with the son's negative attitude, and is in no mood to be patient and wait for a Win/Win opportunity. The parent needs only send him to his room or ground him to the house until he chooses to complete the task as assigned. Then just wait.

Many parents respond to the above notion by asking "What if he won't go to his room?" If dealing with a younger smaller child, escort him to his room; if with an older larger child, warn him that if he refuses to comply he won't like what you do as a result. The next question asked is "Then, what do I do?" One answer is "nothing," and nothing means nothing. The parent doesn't talk, nor instruct, nor order, the parent stops doing laundry, serving meals, giving out money; the parent simply stops doing anything for the child until he goes to the bedroom and then decides to complete the assigned chore.

The parent needs only to be patient and hold out for compliance; if the parent stays calm, the child will eventually choose to comply with the parent's demands, because it will be in his best interest to do so.

Conclusion

The key to making Win/Win Parenting interventions work is for parents to learn to wait and become as insistent upon a child's compliance as she is upon parent to give in. There is no need for parental anger. The child's own sense of need gives the parent control in almost all situations. This naturally leads to cooperation and compliance.

When applied consistently and effectively, Win/Win Parenting is the one parenting tool that provides immediate and irrefutable consequences for noncompliance. When used non-punitively, Win/Win allows the consequences to be chosen in advance by the child. The parent simply has to enforce her part of the contract.

The only ..ay for the intervention to fail is for the parent to give in.

CURFEW VIOLATIONS: TAKE IT ONE DAY AT A TIME ... A DIALOGUE

If your child is late for curfew – and late is late, a minute or hours, it doesn't matter – restrict her to the home for the rest of the day and all of the next.

If the child did not go where she said she was going (she lied), restrict for an extra day.

ONLY ONE DAY?

Yes. Many parents will restrict their children or teenagers for long periods of time (often a week or two) or threaten to do so. One of two things happens: 1) the parent fully enforces the punishment, or 2) the parent gives in.

WHAT IS WRONG WITH ENFORCING ONE OR TWO WEEKS? AFTER ALL, I AM TEACHING MY CHILD THAT HE CAN TRUST ME.

Yes, your child is learning to trust you, but it is also likely that your child is learning to hate and resent you. A week is a long time to a child or teenager. The more they miss, the more they resent you, and the less they remember why they've been restricted in the first place. Also, the longer they're home with you, the more misery they can cause for you by way of blame and anger.

BUT USUALLY HE STRAIGHTENS UP AND I REWARD THIS BY EASING UP ON THE RESTRICTION.

This happens more often than parents are willing to admit, but this type of behavior on the part of the parent encourages mistrust and a false sense of emotional power for the child.

When you change your mind, it is usually because of guilt and/or a desire to end the hassles that the restriction is causing. Simply put, this will result in a broken promise to the child; this creates mistrust. Also, if you relent due the child's behavior, this gives the child a sense of power over you, and can cause the child to take you less seriously in the future.

If you, as the parent, feel that you have been too harsh due to anger, then identify this as such as quickly as possible to the child and reduce the penalty to a more reasonable length of time. Changing things due to the awareness of angry parenting is different than giving into the protestations of an angry child.

BUT WHY ONLY ONE DAY? IS THAT LONG ENOUGH TO TEACH HIM HIS LESSON?

First of all, you need not hurt your child to teach a lesson. Life is hard enough without unnecessary punishments. If you feel the need to inflict pain on your children, then you are modeling the use of pain as punishment, not good parenting. A child will learn from the experience even if only a single day's restriction is used.

It is important for a parent to remember that a large part of parenting is about training the next generation to be parents; parenting should not be about the business of inflicting needless pain to create fear as a way to shape behavior.

HOW DOES JUST ONE DAY TEACH A CHILD TO ADHERE TO CURFEW?

By parental consistency.

WHAT DOES THAT MEAN?

It means that when you say one day, it means one day.

BUT WHAT DOES THE CHILD LEARN, IF HE DOESN'T WANT TO GO ANYWHERE?

He learns that one day means one day.

BUT HOW CAN THIS TEACH ANYTHING? IT SEEMS SO MILD.

Consider that life goes in cycles and that if you are consistent, then the law of averages states that someday when your child is restricted she is going to want to go somewhere very badly (for example, a ball game, concert, party, etc.), but you can now stick to the promise of only one day. The child misses a major event, yet still learns that one day means one day.

WHAT ABOUT TV, TELEPHONE, AND VISITORS?

Disallow them. A child can be permitted to accept phone calls long enough to tell friends that he can't talk because of being grounded; TV time can be earned by doing some task assigned by the parent.

WHAT IF IT DOESN'T WORK?

Then the child will learn to live in the house every other day.

WHAT ABOUT INCREASING IT TO A WEEK OR TWO IF IT DOESN'T WORK?

This is not a good idea, because your child might deliberately test you for consistency, making it possible that things could get worse before they get better. Often, escalating behavior is a sign of resistance to change; you need to hang in there, stand steady, and believe in what you are doing. Remember, behavioral changes occur in children when behavioral changes occur in adults.

Basic Format

- Explain the intervention
- Designate an official clock
- Restrict only for the rest of day and all of the next (unless lying is involved)

- Restrict to the home
- Allow some other freedoms (sometimes parents may allow none depending on circumstances)
- Be consistent; don't relent
- Don't accept excuses

Variations

This intervention can be used throughout childhood after age eight or nine (about the time when children have freer access to the outside world without supervision). This intervention can be applied to youngsters who are old enough to drive a car. Parents don't have to ground their older teenager to the home; they need merely restrict the use of the car for one day when curfew is violated.

HOMEWORK INTERVENTION: AGES 9 THROUGH 15

—ou can lead a horse to water,
but you can't make it learn Algebra.

Parents: Learn —our Limits

Every new school year brings its own set of new problems. Sometimes parents find themselves facing a problem not seen in the past: poor grades.

A typical scenario:

MOTHER: *(with some anticipation)* "Have any homework?"
SON: *(with an air of indifference and cool assuredness)* "Did it at school."
MOTHER: *(with hopeful anxiety)* Good for you."

This scene may be played out nightly, often with variations such as "I did it while you were at work," or "I did it yesterday," or "I didn't have any today," until the interims appear in late September announcing that Johnny is in danger of failing three courses. Mom gets disappointed and angry, then shows the report to dad. Now dad is angry as well. Johnny is grounded for the rest of the quarter. Johnny then gets mad; his grades don't improve and everyone is pretty unhappy about the whole affair.

This type of behavior and response is an example of a typical power struggle between parents and children. It is a struggle that the parents can't win, because the goal of good grades is unattainable for them; good grades are the child's option, not theirs.

In the case above, the parents were doing the only thing they knew: punishing Johnny. But there are other options. What follows is a recommendation for dealing with poor grades that is not punitive, and it works.

- Inform the youngster that she will have a study period each night before a school day for the rest of the year. This study period can be as short as half an hour and as long as two hours. Initially, it is recommended that a medium length of time be used (about one hour) to allow for some flexibility that will be useful later. However, once the parent selects the length of the study period, it can only be changed after the youngster's performance at school changes; do not give in to protestations that, on any given evening, something else might be more important than the study period.

  If the child starts griping and arguing with about this parental decision, let her know that you are willing to go back to the old method of total restriction until the end of the quarter.

- This study period will take place at the dining room or kitchen table, and there will be no radio, television, talking, or sleeping.

- There will be books present at the table that are deemed to be educational (by the parent).

  If no books are brought home, one can be provided by the parent; the length of the study period can be extended by fifteen minutes as a consequence (and motivator). If books are not brought home, various writings can be assigned from various texts as a substitute. Consider the Declaration of Independence, the Magna Carta, the Constitution of the United States, Bible chapters and verses, Shakespeare plays, etc.

- The youngster must remain awake and at least appear to be studying. If there is some question about the child's sincerity, stop the time and note that the time will resume when she looks busy. When you first introduce the notion of a study time to the youngster, be sure to inform him that if his grades improve, the study time will be shortened. If not, the study time will be increased. Then, if he is carrying on about how unfair you are, just remind him that the old intervention of ongoing grounding until the next report period is still an option (as noted above).

- ***Do not try to make the youngster study***; just enforce the study time. If you, as a parent, simply enforce the study time, then you have done your job. The rest will be up to your child.

- When the study time is over, it is over; there are no subsequent sanctions. Avoid monitoring the progress of the child while doing his homework, but be certain to remain available should he or she request your help.

Parents should note that the intent of this intervention is to provide children with the opportunity to study, and to provide parents with the satisfaction that they have done what they can do to promote good grades. It is of the utmost importance that parents avoid a power struggle in which grades become the major issue or weapon.

Finally, it is important to remember: Some kids need to know that they are loved as failures before they are willing to go on to succeed.

THE DRIVER'S LICENSE: A GUIDE FOR RESPONSIBLE PARENTING

The material that follows is a structured approach to dealing with an adolescent's desire to obtain a driver's permit and operator's license. It should be noted that there are two very distinct sets of criteria for successfully attaining driving privileges: your state's rules and your own particular rules for your child and situation.

ABOUT THE STATE'S RULES

Although the rules for each state vary somewhat with regard to age and driving requirements, each state has a codified set of expectations for achieving and maintaining a driver's license. Parents should be careful to make sure that they do as little as possible to assist their child in getting the license. The more legwork (i.e., information acquisition, financial considerations, and other logistical matters) that is left up to the youngster, the better informed will be the parents about the desire and willingness of the child to be responsible for his or her own "right" to drive a car.

Each state has a procedure that each youth must successfully endure in order to become a licensed driver. When considering their role in matters of gaining the driving privilege, parents must ask themselves the question:

"Is this material vital to me or to my child?" Parents should answer this question along the lines of recognizing that the youngster is the one who needs to know what to do about getting a driver's license, not the parent. Thus, the parent can tell the teen to figure out what he or she needs to do. If the child comes up with viable answers for that part of the process, then the parent knows that the child is motivated and willing to do some work to get the license. If the child sits around and does nothing except bemoan the fact that "it's too much for me, I can't understand all of this legal stuff;" then the parent can conclude the kid is not ready to drive yet.

There will be things in the process that only a parent will be able to provide (e.g., a ride to the license agency; accompany the youth when getting hours of driving experience while holding a temporary permit; permission to take driver's education, and etc.), but outside of those things that can only be performed by the parent, the child should lead the way. His or her behavior and choices will reveal his or her readiness for driving.

Lastly, parents *should* know the rules of their state. They should know the rules for all of the stages for the acquisition process, but they should get this information from their children. There is no need for the parent to go out and seek the driver's education laws of their state when there is a youngster who is supposed to be motivated to obtain that very education and its reward. When a parent lets the youngster do the work of getting the license, greater assurance of readiness can be ascertained from the youth's behavior in the process.

Mom and Dad's Basic Rules: Your Law

Once a teen has successfully obtained the materials necessary to initiate the licensing process, parents will need to present a clear set of expectations in order for the young person to gain permission to move on with the process. What follows is a set of guidelines that can be modified to suit the needs of and parent and child's particular situation.

GETTING THE PERMIT (AKA: THE TEMPORARY LICENSE)

When a young person is motivated to obtain a learner's permit to operate a motor vehicle, he or she should:

- Maintain satisfactory grade point average in school for the two quarters prior to the minimum age for obtaining the temporary permit to learn to drive. These requirements will vary according to the potential of the individual teen, but should be clearly defined and rigidly maintained. It is recommended that parents set requirements such as a 3.0 average with no C's, or a 2.0 average with no D's. However, it is of the utmost importance that whatever standard is set for the teen, the standard be fully met and not compromised by the parents for "making a good try." Driving a car is one of the most serious activities taken on by a young person; it is the parents' prerogative and responsibility to make certain the youngster is fully ready to accept this awesome challenge.

- Maintain satisfactory behavioral decorum for three months prior to obtaining the learner's permit. This means no serious (i.e., destructive) temper losses or suicidal gestures for the three months prior to the minimum age of getting the permit.

  Parents should set clear guidelines for the kinds of behaviors that are and are not acceptable for a young person who wishes to drive. In cases where the teens display problems with dangerous rage or suicidal tendencies, parents can reset the three month clock immediately after a serious behavioral episode. In other words, if the youth displays a serious fit of rage, he has to wait three months before getting his permit. Driving a car is an adult privilege; parents need to be realistic about refusing to allow an emotionally or behaviorally disordered teen get behind the wheel of a vehicle of potential disaster.

- Be behaviorally and financially responsible for obtaining the permit (she must do the legwork and pay for the permit). This means, also, that the teen should have some financial accountability in securing driver's education. This could be as little as ten percent of the total cost of the lessons, but the actual amount is not nearly as important as is the parents' refusal to pay the remaining balance until the youth puts up her end of the money. This is another way parents can measure the sincerity and maturity of their teen with regard to obtaining the driving privilege.

A WORD OF CAUTION

Many young people are responsible and reliable people, but if a young person has a long standing history of failed follow-through at home and school, then the parent of that child should be careful when it comes to granting the license. Many a young person will promise to make significant changes when he or she is about to enter the process of getting a driver's license; parents of these youngsters must be especially careful to set and maintain clear expectations for these types of youngsters. Nothing magical happens the day a young person turns 16; he is still the same as he has been all along; character does not change because of a birthday. Rather character matures over time (usually over an extended period) as a child meets up with the rigors of "real life." When "real life" is allowed to affect a child's development, that child will learn to adapt to life's demands; but when parents routinely intervene, intercede, or interfere with the forces of life on a child's behalf, there is the greatest of chances that the youngster will fail to develop a healthy character.

Parents should be very exacting regarding a youngster's compliance with conditions for obtaining and maintaining the driving privilege. It is much easier to set and maintain strict and demanding terms from the beginning of the process than it is to attempt to set and enforce more stringent terms after a youngster has already been indulged in the driving process.

Note: As children become familiar with driving, parents come to rely on the youngster's ability to drive as a great help to parents themselves; in matters of discipline, parents must refrain from letting the child's driving privilege become the parent's need rather than the teen's. When the time comes, it is best to pull the privilege rather than promote an air of indulgence.

A WORD ABOUT INSURANCE DURING THE LEARNING PERIOD

When a youngster holds a temporary permit to drive, he or she is usually covered under the insurance of the parents' carrier. However, it makes sense for the youngster to be directed to contact the insurance carrier to confirm that this is so, and to give the youth practice at being behaviorally responsible the driving process.

GETTING THE LICENSE

Once the requirements for the temporary driver's license have been met, the youngster then has to move forward to getting his probationary license. The concept of "probationary" as it pertains to any particular household and state needs to be explained to the new driver.

The young person should:

- Maintain grades (as were required for getting the permit) throughout the learning period.

- Know and keep all state requirements for obtaining the license; parents should never make allowances for work not completed during the learning period, nor should the parents agree to cheat on the hourly requirements which may be demanded by the state "because he's really a good driver."

- Avoid any violation of the rules as set forth by the state; serious violations (even though not caught by state officials) should carry a mandatory 30 day delay in obtaining the license. Repeated serious infractions should be met with a complete denial of driving privileges until the youth demonstrates satisfactory maturity or is old enough to meet the state's requirements without parental endorsement.

Remember, parents may be held responsible (see your state laws and/or codes) for acts committed by their children while operating a motor vehicle when holding a probationary driver's license.

MAINTAINING THE LICENSE

Teens between the ages of sixteen and eighteen who have earned their licenses need to be reminded that their license is a privilege granted by their parents and their state of residence.

- Maintain grades (as were required for getting the permit) throughout the learning period.

- Be financially responsible for maintaining some portion of the insurance costs, or should be making some payment each month toward the cost of the car they drive. Again, this will help the parent assess the level of behavioral commitment the child has for maintaining his driving privilege. When stipulations for driving remain unmet, parents must be willing to withdraw the driving privilege until the terms are fulfilled. Remember, if a child is old enough to drive a car, he or she is old enough to walk or use public transportation when driving privileges have been lost.

- Maintain household responsibilities such as routine chores or requests made by parents for help around the house. Teens between 16 and 18 need no longer be grounded for unacceptable behaviors, especially if they are driving. Parents can simply remove the driving privilege for a few days, and allow the youngster to feel the humility of having to get around without wheels. (Parents need to refrain from feeling responsible for getting the youth to work or other activities out of a sense of guilt and obligation; let the youth worry about this.) It is not a parent's duty to operate a taxi service when a young person has lost his or her driving privilege.

Please Note: Parents should not overly employ the restriction of driving privileges as a way to get a teen to conform to large numbers of parental expectations. Removal of driving privileges should be reserved for matters of blatant disrespect of the parent's authority or disrespect of the driving privilege itself.

When a parent is struggling to gain cooperation in completing household chores or with compliance regarding financial commitments, the driving privilege needs only be denied UNTIL the situation at hand is remedied by the young person (see Win/Win Parenting p. 156).

Who Owns the Car? Ages 16 and 17

Many parents want to buy their kids a first car just so they don't have to let the kid use mom's or dad's late model vehicle.

There can be a major downside to this generous distribution of wealth, if the youth does not earn the ownership of this vehicle. Often a teen will come to expect to have the car at anytime for any reason, and will regard the car as his own with little or no restriction. Often, for a variety of reasons, parents will find themselves backpedaling to try to regain some control over the use of the vehicle. When these situations arise, the youth will recoil with a great deal of anger and indignation over the loss of what is perceived to be a right (i.e., an entitlement).

Parents can reduce the entitlement factor often associated with a car and a youth by constructing ways for the young person to earn the right to claim ownership of the car. Parents of means are sometimes loathe to require their children to go to work, and for some it is a symbol of their own wealth to be able to afford to provide a late model (or even new) car for their youngster to drive (own).

Many parents will provide a car to their teen on the condition that the teen will keep up grades, chores and other demands, and the youngster will be all too happy to agree. The problem comes later when the parent is used to having a teen who is somewhat self-sufficient, but irresponsible with regard to keeping those earlier promises. The parent then finds it difficult to remove the car because the child now sees that the car as a right, and the notions of privilege and responsibility goes out the window. It is in the best interests of a young person for that young person to be challenged with having to pay (either with work, grades, or money) for the car he or she drives. Many parents find out much too late that indulgence comes with a price, and that price is a weakened character that lacks depth, substance and determination.

In most family situations, even those in which a minor child is working to pay for a car, parents should insist that the youngster understand that the ownership of the vehicle is actually controlled by the parents, and that the rights to this vehicle can be revoked by the parents for various durations at anytime for violation of driving laws and basic household rules (e.g., curfew, drug and alcohol use, school attendance and performance, and serious behavioral problems). Yet it is the youngster's responsibility to maintain the car, gas it up, keep tires on it, and so forth. If it breaks down, it is the responsibility of the youngster to get it fixed (or at least help).

Parents should not step forward to rescue their teen from the financial rigors of early adulthood. Some parents think that their child cannot afford to take on the financial responsibility of owning and driving a car; if this is the case, then these parents can rethink whether or not the teen should be able to claim ownership to the car. In these situations parents should revert to a more dependent arrangement where the parent owns the car, and the youngster gets to use it only when permission is given.

More About Insurance

When any parent agrees to pay for the costs of maintaining a young person's car insurance, it is likely that the youth will be less apt to realize the serious nature of driving a car, nor will he have an understanding of the work it takes to participate in real life. It is against the law of most states for anyone to drive an automobile without minimum liability insurance. Driving a car is an adult privilege that requires enormous responsibility; children ought not to be driving automobiles. When a parent insists that a youngster obtains her own insurance in order to drive (or pays some percentage of the premium), that parent can be better assured that the youth is responsible enough to handle the privilege.

Please note: If a youngster is making a car payment every month, there is nothing wrong with the parent picking up the tab for the insurance (or supplying the car if the youngster pays the insurance), but it is important to remember that the willingness to surrender money to obtain a freedom or to realize a desire is a reflection of maturation in our society. Sacrifice does build character.

Conclusion

No matter what choices parents make for responding to the "car issue," parents should remember two things: first and foremost, driving a car is a serious responsibility that can be life threatening, and second, parents will have to live with the consequences of their actions with their young drivers. There are no guarantees that good parenting will result in safe driving, but it can be safely said that irresponsible parenting greatly increases the risk for irresponsible driving.

BIBLIOGRAPHY

Cline, Foster W., M.D., *Hope for High Risk and Rage Filled Children,* EC Publications, Evergreen Colorado, 1992

Kaufman, Gershen, Shame: *The Power of Caring,* Third edition, Schenkman Books, Inc.; Rochester, Vermont; 1992.

Kaufman, Gershen, *The Psychology of Shame; Theory and Treatment of Shame-based Syndromes,* Springer Publishing Company; New York; 1989.

Mahler, Margaret; Pine, Fred, Bergman, Anni;, *Psychological Birth of the Human Infant,* Basics Books, Inc.; New York; 1975.

Reich, Wilhelm; Higgins, Mary B.; Chester M. Md. Waphael (Editor), *Reich Speaks of Freud: Wilhelm Reich Discusses His Work and His Relationship With Sigmund Freud,* Farrar, Straus, and Giroux, New York.

Winnicott, D.W., *Home is Where We Start From, 'Essays by a Psychoanalyst,'* W.W. Norton and Company, 1986.

SELECTED READING LIST

Cline, Foster W., M.D.; Fay, James, *Parenting with Love and Logic,* Pinion Press, 1990.

Cline, M.D., Foster; Fay, Jim; *Parenting Teens with Love and Logic,* Pinion Press, 1992.

Dreikurs, M.D., Rudolf; Soltz, R.N., Vicki, *Children: The Challenge,* Hawthorn Books (Original publication), New York; 1964.

Friedman, Edwin H., *Friedman's Fables,* The Guilford Press, New York,1990.

Karen, Robert, *Shame,* The Atlantic Monthly Magazine, February 1992.

Satir, Virginia, *People Making,* Science and Behavior Books; 1988.

Welch, Martha; *Holding Time: How to Eliminate Conflict, Temper Tantrums, and Sibling Rivalry, and Raise Happy, Loving, Successful Children,* A Fireside Book published by Simon and Schuster, New York, 1988.

Winnicott, D. W., *Human Nature,* Schocken Books, Inc., New York, 1988.

ISBN 1-41205314-5